ORIENTAL
BIRTH
DREAMS

ORIENTAL
BIRTH
DREAMS

by

FRED JEREMY SELIGSON

HOLLYM

First published
by Hollym International Corp.
18 Donald Place
Elizabeth, New Jersey 07208 U.S.A.

Published simultaneously in Korea
by Hollym Corporation; Publishers
14-5 Kwanchol-dong, Chongno-gu, Seoul, Korea
Phone: (02)735-7554   FAX: (02)730-5149

ISBN : 0-930878-67-1
Library of Congress Catalogue Card Number: 89-83651

Printed in Korea

This is a Love Letter to the World

FOREWORD

In recent decades, the Western world has been discovering the legacy of dream tradition and the rich inheritance that has been dream-deeded to the current generation of dream explorers. By contemplating the characters, scenery, and events they encounter during their nocturnal odysseys, dreamers have found that they can illuminate new areas of self-awareness that previously had remained in darkness.

This awakening to the potential of our dreaming minds has been accompanied by increased efforts to understand the possible role that somatic factors may play in the production of nocturnal dreams. In the United States, several recent dissertations and the book, *Dream Worlds of Pregnancy*, have investigated the special nature of pregnant women's dreams and what significance they might possess for both mother and child. Some of these studies suggest that particular types of dreams during pregnancy may portend certain outcomes related to length of labor, possible birth deformities, or subsequent physical welfare of the baby.

Another direction being followed by modern dream research has been the effort to carry out cross-cultural studies dealing with the dream beliefs and practices of non-Western societies. Many critics have complained that Freud allowed his dream theories to be overdetermined by the Victorian Viennese culture in which he was raised and in which he practiced. Access to the alternative views held in other cultures about various dream phenomena can help minimize the possibility of ethnocentric bias.

All these issues—the legacy of dream tradition, the significance of pregnancy dreams, and the influence of cultural beliefs—are masterfully joined in this book by Professor Seligson. He is to be congratulated for compiling this superb collection of Oriental birth dreams.

His survey of the way birth dreams were viewed in earlier times in the Orient and how they still are given great prominence by modern Korea and nearby countries, documents the international status of our dream legacy. Readers with an inclination toward research can ferret out some hypotheses to explore with regard to examining the validity of the proposed connections between specific dream imagery and the predicted outcomes claimed to be associated with them. Those with a theoretical bent can attempt to propose how culturally ingrained beliefs can serve to manifest certain forms of dream mentation in response to altered physiological functioning which accompanies pregnancy. For the large number of people who are content with simple dream appreciation, reading through some of these beautiful and poignant dreams will serve as a reminder of just how diverse and delightful our dreaming minds can be. I am grateful for Professor Seligson's labors, and I hope this book that he has delivered will have a long and auspicious life.

Robert L. Van de Castle, Ph.D.
Professor of Behavioral Medicine and Psychiatry
University of Virginia Medical School
Former President of the Association for the Study of Dreams

CONTENTS

9

CONTENTS

PART THREE
DREAM ZOOS

PART FOUR
DREAMS OF GODS AND HUMANS

CONTENTS

PART FIVE
DREAM TREASURES

PART SIX
AN INTERPRETATION OF BIRTH DREAMS

ACKNOWLEDGMENTS

I would like to thank the many friends who have freely helped this dream come true.

Among them are Lee Jae-hyung, an eighty year old Taoist, who shared his wisdom.

Han Yoon-ki who painted most of the lovely illustrations.

Young-suk Loeding, who while pregnant, typed the original manuscript, and her husband, Dave, who taught me word processing.

David Kosofsky, John Porter and Thomas Shroyer who contributed to the editing.

Students Jang Doe-her, Quon Son-chol, Lee Chung-su, Lee Jin-suk, Lee Joo-seong, Lee Tae-hyung, and Lee Won-suk who translated for me.

Professors Kim Yol-gyu, Kim Young-jo, Kim Young-ok, Lee Kyu-yoon, and Min Man-shik who advised me.

Kim Yong-tae M.D., Rhi Bou-yong M.D., and Kim Hong-kyeong O.M.D. who offered me medical insights.

Colleagues Kumatani Akiyasu, Miyata Hisashi and Nobohiro Shinji of Japan; Chang Shao-wen, Wang Su-yi and Yang Rur-bin of Taiwan; and Ali Balaman of Turkey who lent me cross-cultural comparisons.

Paik Syeung-gil of Korea UNESCO and his editors who encouraged me by publishing my articles on birth dreams.

Rhimm In-soo, Chu Shin-won, and editors Kim Kwang-suk, and Om Kyong-hui at Hollym Corporation, Publishers who at last made this book a reality.

I am especially grateful to my wife, Young-im, who shared her folklore and love.

INTRODUCTION

The hand belongs to the region of the lesser Yin. When the motion of her pulse is great, she is with child.

(The Yellow Emperor's Classic, Veith trs.)

Sitting by old, Mr. Lee Jae-hyung in his hill-top tent, I asked, "Where do birth dreams come from?"

He stared at me a while and said, "Do you really want to know?"

"Of course."

Then he opened his tobacco box and began rolling a herb and tiger bone cigarette, which he licked, stuck at the end of a horn, and lit... "According to the Five Elements' Theory of the *Yellow Emperor's Classic of Internal Medicine,*" he answered, "a blue (green) dragon is compared with the liver. The liver keeps blood. Our blood moves with energy and circulates to the five organs.

"It goes to the kidneys turning black. Goes to the lungs turning white. Goes to the heart turning red. Goes to the spleen turning yellow. Goes to the liver again and turns green. Thus, as it circulates blood changes color."

"Is that true?," I exclaimed in disbelief.

"Yes," he replied, and took a puff.

He went on, "A dream comes from a lack of energy, intestinal activity, or frustrations. When energy is lacking, the five organs cannot act properly, so a dream comes out.

"When liver vitality is lacking, we can see this condition in our dreams. Green trees and grass appear on hills, for example.

"If the heart has frustrations, we dream of the color red, like in a forest fire.

"If the lungs are weak with grief, we fly in our dreams and see white.

"When the spleen suffers from worry, we see yellow, perhaps a swamp.

"And when the kidneys are failing out of fear, we see dark waters in our dreams.

"Is that true, too?" I couldn't help but say.

He stared at me, and spat out some juice into an old tin can. "Of course."

"So why does a woman have a baby dream?" Mr. Lee continued, "If she conceives before she has a dream, then the colors of fruits and vegetables, and the appearance of mountains, heavenly bodies and so on in the dreams are related to the lack of activity of the organs.

"Upon conception, a baby's physical structure is composed only of *yang* fire. Its body collects its mother's energy and brings it to the womb to feed on. So the energy of all five organs becomes empty and collects in only one place, the womb.

"From this time on the future mother appears tired and sick and sometimes throws up. Her limbs are weak and she lies down on the floor.

"This is why women always have dreams while pregnant. But after conception a dream is useless, 'a dog's dream.'"

The lines around his eyes stretched like rays of the sun as he laughed out loud and said, "Before, or just upon conception, a woman can have a real prophetic dream! A real birth dream never expends her energy. She still preserves all her energy.

"Just as the 'ghosts' of Heaven's and those of the woman's body join together and crystallize to make a baby, so does a birth dream occur when Heaven's 'ghost' enters the mother's body."

Bathing
in a stream, alone
in the moonlight,
I saw a red pepper
floating around me.

Without thinking,
I picked it out of the water,
and woke up.

Ten months later
I had a gentle,
tho obstinate, boy.

(Korean woman's dream)

These are stories about love....

Love is the source of birth and of the dreams which reveal the conception, sex and destinies of children who may be just entering the womb.

Long ago, it may have been that no one could be born into this world without such a dream forecasting his or her birth. This was believed true not only of future saints, heroes and other gifted persons, but of ordinary children as well.

It was true of Buddha, whose mother Maya dreamt a beautiful, six-tusked white elephant ran, trumpeting loudly into the palace and around her bed three times. It plunged into her womb through the right side of her ribs.

(See Part Three, Dream Zoos.)

It was true of Alexander the Great, whose mother Olympias dreamed she was sleeping with Ammon, the horned god of Libya; and Alexander's father, Philip, dreamed of seeing an imperial seal with the figure of a lion on his wife's womb.

Likewise, it was true of Augustus Caesar, whose mother Atia dreamed that "her intestines were being carried up to the stars and stretched over all lands and seas."

It was also true of Mary's husband, Joseph, who dreamed;

...the angel of the Lord appeared unto him..., saying "Joseph, thou son of David, fear not to take unto thee of the Holy Ghost.

And she shall bring forth a son, and thou shall call him JESUS: for he shall save his people from their sins..."

(*Matthew* 1:18-24)

With a birth dream, a child could be inspired to fulfill great promise; be a mystical saint, an entertainer with the spirit of a rainbow, a general as ferocious as a tiger, a scholar as keen and pure as a crane, or an Olympic hero with legs like a deer. His life could be as long as a spool of white thread. Or if a girl, she could be as pretty as a peony.

If a white-bearded god, or a "heaven girl" had appeared in the dream, he or she would continue protecting and nurturing the child throughout its life.

My Korean teacher of the esoteric, Mr. Lee Jae-hyung, says, "Orientals believed that no baby could be born without a birth dream, or if it was, it was sure to die soon,

Ch'ima An ample Korean skirt, called a *ch'ima* represents the womb.
Korean ladies hide the secrets of their birth dreams in their *ch'imas*.

T'aegŭk Butterfly The *T'aegŭk* (Great Ultimate) butterfly, symbolizing the female and male forces of change in the universe, flits through every dreamer's heart.

The Yongwang (Dragon King), holding a magical pearl in his hand, is surrounded by two of his dragons.

Buddha's Mother's Dream While Queen Maya was sleeping, this white elephant entered her ribs, on the right in a dream. Sakyamuni, the future Buddha was conceived.

Baby Buddha raises a finger, showing us the oneness of all beings.

The Sanshin (Mountain God) and his awesome servant, the tiger, rule over the creatures of the land. The god appears in people's dreams, bearing the gift of a child. The tiger, a frequent visitor in dreams, usually promises a son.

Thatched House It's a simple country dwelling, thatched with rice straw, but modern Koreans wish to, and so do return here in their dreams.

Banquet given on a Baby's First Birthday (An anonymous genre painting, Yi dynasty, 1392-1910).

Shin Saimdang (1512–1559) was the mother of Yi Yul-gok, a distinguished Neo-Confucianist. She dreamed of an awesome dragon before giving birth to her son.

Yi Sun-shin (1545–1598) was an innovative admiral who saved the Choson kingdom from a Japanese invasion. His mother dreamed of a young man supporting a falling tree.

Min-bi (1851-1895) was the ambitious, last queen of the Yi dynasty. She was assassinated by Japanese agents. Her mother dreamed of a scarlet cloud.

An Chung-gŭn (1879–1910) was a young revolutionary who assassinated Itō Hirobumi, the Japanese governor of Korea. His father dreamed of a frightened tiger.

Korean Flag The round *T'aegŭk* and the I-Ching trigrams for Heaven ☰ and Earth ☷, Fire ☲ and Water ☵ on the Korean flag, provide keys for the interpretation of birth dreams. They imprint images of the shadowy, female *yin* and the bright, male *yang* forces of nature on the collective dream mind of the Korean people.

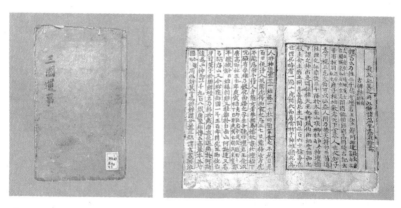

Samguk Yusa This book written by the monk, Ilyŏn in the Koryŏ period (918–1392) relates the history of ancient Korean kingdoms. The *Samguk Yusa* contains many legends and myths, including the birth dream of Kim Suro, the founder of Kaya, which continue to influence the dreams of modern Koreans.

or be deformed, or mentally defective, because it had no spiritual blessing." This was thought true, at least in pre-modern countries influenced by classical Chinese culture such as Korea and Vietnam.

In China, such dreams are called *t'aimeng*, and in Korea, *t'aemong*. The Chinese character *t'ai* means "womb," "foetus," or "unborn child," and *meng* means "dream." Together they mean "a predictive dream about an unborn child."

Such a dream can be dreamt not only by the mother, but also occasionally by the father, grandparents, in-laws, siblings or even friends of the mother.

In response to my query, "Where do birth dreams come from?," Mr. Lee, who traveled in China long before the 1949 Revolution, told me,

"The tradition of birth dreams is very old, dating back 12,000 years in China. One example of a Chinese birth dream concerns Huang-ti, the 'Yellow Emperor' (2696–2598 B.C.), who was the father of Chinese medicine. His mother dreamed a yellow dragon jumped into her throat, and suddenly she woke up, surprised."

"So you mean birth dreams came from China?," I said.

"That's right. Korea inherited them from China, and later transmitted them to Japan..."

Continuing to trace the tradition in China, from the early part of the Chou Dynasty (1122–256 B.C.), a poem in the *Book of Poetry* (*She King*) (translated by James Legge) describes an elaborate residence and bed-chamber, and how it has been built to suit the dreams of the king, Suen. In the 6th verse, it reads:

> *On the rush mat below, and that of fine bamboos above it.*

17

Here may he repose in slumber!
May he sleep and awake,
(Saying) "Divine for me dreams.
What dreams are lucky ?
They have been of bears and grisly bears;
They have been of cobras and (other) serpents."

He knows his dreams are special, having a "heavenly"
message, but he requires a trained interpreter, a diviner.

The chief diviner will divine them.
The bears and grisly bears
Are the auspicious intimations of sons.
The cobras and (other) serpents
Are the auspicious intimations of daughters.

Bears are sons, and serpents (especially small or rainbow ribboned ones) are daughters in Korea, too.

Sons shall be born to him.
They will be put to sleep on couches;
They will be clothed in robes;
They will have scepters to play with;
Their cry will be loud.
They will be (hereafter) resplendent with red
knee-covers,
The (future) king, the princes of the land.

Sons are seen as being "precious" in Korea, too.

Daughters shall be born to him.
They will be put to sleep on the ground;
They will be clothed in wrappers.
They will have tiles to play with.
It will be their's neither to do wrong nor to do
good.
Only about the spirits and the food will they have
to think,
And to cause no sorrow to their parents.

Daughters in Korea too, until recently, were considered of little value.

It is not just accidental that the Chinese and Korean traditions are similar. Chinese visited early Korean kingdoms, and Korean soldiers, diplomats, scholars, and monks visited neighboring China, and, or studied Chinese culture at home, doubtlessly learning about the birth dreams of famous Chinese. Some of these were probably circulated by word of mouth throughout ordinary Korean society, influencing both the motivation for, and content of people's birth dreams.

While in Honolulu, during the summer of '86, I looked up Peter H. Lee, a thin, white-haired professor of Korean Studies (now at UCLA), and asked him, "Where do Korean birth dreams come from?" He, the child of a dream about a "scholarly crane," acknowledged some Chinese influence, but, gazing at me with a light which kind of penetrated my soul, added that, "All over the world, birth dreams probably arose out of man's roots in nature, and this was so in Korea, too.

"The old tribes and clans of Shilla had totems. One such totem was a cock; others were a tiger and a bear, and these influenced the images in birth dreams. In other words, our people's ancestors were animals, or at least believed to be animals."

Koreans and other early Asian peoples' ancestors were not only animals, but plants and inanimate objects, too. These, like humans, were believed to have metamorphic spirits which could leave their sleeping bodies and roam the world of night, sometimes entering into a sleeping woman's womb to become the seed of her child. Instinctively, the stone-age woman would open her eyes of dream and mystically participate with the visiting soul in a paradise of the "dawn of man." Upon awakening, she would know that she was with child.

Today in Asia, just as in prehistoric times, when the first signs of pregnancy are unconsciously detected, a vivid and unforgettable dream spontaneously arises to inform a woman that she is with child. The dream arises out of a pool of naturalistic images, from her own personal and inherited memories, and her own mind metamorphoses it into hills, valleys, dragons and pearls. She is a metamorphic being, as all humans are; for she is split into several selves, which come alive, however fleetingly, on a dream landscape long enough for her to commune with and confirm her child-to-be, who has come from "another world" in order to choose and possess an identifying image of its own.

She bathes
in a clear stream,
secluded by scented
trees, under glowing sun.

While in paradise,
a tiger enters her womb,
and she sets a moonstone
on her finger.

A star falls
on her breast.

She snips lilies
into the folds
of her dress

going home
with her child.

In modern Europe and America, belief in such dreams is rare, something of the mythological past; the inherited mythology in dreams only occasionally functions as a birth prophecy. Some Westerners, however, do have pre-cognitive birth dreams, and though they may be quite poetic, they are of a more individual nature, lacking the unified cultural antiquity of Oriental ones. Here is an example of an American woman's lovely dream:

> I saw a little girl
> with ivy growing out of her head,
> just like an elf.
>
> I bore a little girl
> who had no hair for years,
> and was just like an elf
> in appearance.

(Katheryn Bennett, Santa Fe, New Mexico)

Her dream shows obvious European, possibly Celtic influence and though scattered Americans do have such mythologically influenced birth dreams, perhaps only among some American Indian tribes has there been a cohesive living prophetic tradition of birth dreams. A remarkable example of this is given by anthropologist Kenneth M. Steward:

"The religions of the River (Colorado) Yumans centered around a most unusual conception of prenatal dreaming, in which the unborn soul of the dreamer was projected back in time to the scene of creation, where power was conferred by the deities. Not all people had 'great dreams,' but power for success as a warrior, a chief, a shaman, or a singer had to be dreamed rather than learned."

As in Asia, such dreams were supposed to be kept secret by the dreamer. Telling them could reduce or even

21

lose the magical power of a birth dream. So it is said by the Yumans, "If a man tells his dream it passes with the day." Similarly my Korean student's mother told him, "Why do you ask me for your birth dream? A birth dream is your life. Why do you ask me for your life?"

Along like lines of secrecy, a Korean high school teacher said, "When I was ten or eleven years old my mother told me, 'I had a good birth dream about you.'

"I said, 'Tell me about it.'

"She refused to, saying, 'If I tell you now, the dream will be destroyed, but it was good and you will be a great man.'

"I didn't ask her again, but I continued wondering, 'What did she dream?'

"When I was sixteen, my mother died. I couldn't ask anybody about the dream because she hadn't told anyone. I was anxious to know about her dream. Some days later, however, I dreamed that my mother appeared and showed me my birth dream. It was made up of three vivid parts, but I can't tell you about it now."

(Mr. Yu)

Younger people, however, are usually much more willing to disclose their dreams. Until recently, in rural Korea, where doctors were few and far between, often the earliest sign of conception, and only indication of an unborn child's sex, was a biologically coincidental dream message from a "living" source of creation, an entity such as "God," or "Heaven," with which we, its children, are intimately connected.

A birth dream is also possibly a "shared" dream, on a common dreamscape, originating in the minds of both a newly arriving baby's "spirit" and its dreaming mother.

A mother thinks of her dreams throughout pregnancy, imprinting images on the foetus in her womb. Even after birth she harbors the secret of her child in prayers for his or her well-being and success.

Then, at the end of the line, the same, but more aged image will arise and depart through the door of life, maybe in a near one's dream, to find a new home.

My purpose in putting this book together is to preserve a treasury of Oriental birth dreams, which are disappearing now, due to modern life-styles, western psychological and religious beliefs and communism. This particularly is the case in China, Japan, and Taiwan, where they are generally thought of as "superstitious." Living in Korea, however, where birth dreams are still believed in, I have had access to specimens of inspiring beauty.

This book is composed of numerous dreams I have gathered with the help of my students at the Hankuk University of Foreign Studies, in Seoul. Out of 2000 dreams, I have chosen about 200 of the most vivid ones, which also give pictures of traditional Korean life. They read like magical prose poems, and open up a unique "other world" preceding our births. Several of the dreams are recorded history from China, India and Japan. Most are from Korea, for they represent perhaps the finest "living" example of the traditional dream culture of the Orient. They form a collective dream myth of creation for the Korean people, with obvious roots reaching back to Imperial China, Buddhist India, and the wilds of animistic, northeast Asian tribes.

Part One

A PANORAMA OF DREAMS

Childless women gaze up in spring at twinkling stars, bursting clouds, or blossoming trees, and pray fervently to be inspired with new life in their wombs.

The long months of concentration of their desires for a child, preferably a son in the Orient, reach the sympathetic, though invisible ears of baby "spirits," who visit in their dreams.

Invisibly, invisibly,
living visibly,
I am the dream
of being reborn

Into "this world,"
a ball of light,
wearing clothes
of dreams
and flesh,
and out
like one too

Visibly, visibly
dying invisibly,
yet on the way
of being reborn.

Usually there is no doubt in a dreamer's mind when she (or he) has a birth dream, and it is so vivid and revealing that she can never forget it.

It normally starts with her washing clothes or bathing in a stream, drawing water from a well, or setting out on an unknown quest in the beauty of nature, often near her current or girlhood home.

She passes over paradisiacal fields, by streams or lakes, climbs up forested mountains or down valleys until she encounters the "baby symbol," or disguised, baby's "spirit," which is generally an object associated with the real or imagined daily life of her native region of China, Korea, or Japan.

With such a symbol, because of prior experiences with similar objects, it is possible that she may already have an intimate, emotional tie.

If her husband is a fisherman, the symbol may be a fish. Or if her home is in a potato-growing area, it might be a potato. Or the baby's "spirit" also could be embodied by a god, an owl, a ginseng root, a diamond or any number of natural forms.

During her encounter with the baby symbol, she may enclose it in her hand, wrap it up in her billowy Korean skirt, swallow it, absorb it through her bosom, belly, or even vagina (symbolically implanting it in her womb), and then merrily bring it home.

When she wakes up, the wondrous vision is still before her eyes and she is amazed. Excitedly, she shakes her husband awake, and pours out the news, or runs to tell her mother, or mother-in-law about it, in hopes of confirming the dream as a prophecy of a coveted child, especially a son.

Any symbol, however, according to the customary, Oriental *yin* (feminine) and *yang* (masculine) particulars of the dream, can signify a girl(女) or a boy(男). For this reason, it is often necessary to consult a professional fortuneteller.

Yin and *yang* are household words in the Orient for the opposite, but complementary active and passive forces of nature. Simply speaking, the shadowy side of a hill is called *yin* and the bright side *yang*; the play of dark and light make up a whole. All phenomena in nature are created through an interaction of the forces of *yin* and *yang*, and this process is symbolized by the blue and red, egg-like *T'aegŭk* symbol of Taoism and Confucianism which also beautifies the Korean flag. *Yin* is composed of water, cold, wet, low, heavy, sinking, hidden, timid and tame qualities and when attached to a baby symbol in a birth dream means a girl will be born. *Yang* is paired with the above by fire, hot, dry, high, light, rising, open, bold and wild qualities and indicates the birth of a boy. Every dreaming mother (and father) houses the age-old *yin/yang* symbol in the center of her (his) heart and all subtle messages of forthcoming conception, be they from supernatural or psycho-biological sources, are filtered through it to announce the sex of an unborn child. These concepts are keys for your own interpretation of the following birth dreams.

HEAVENLY DREAMS

Suns
and moons

are brothers
and sisters

rising
and setting,

setting,
rising.

SUN

In ancient China, Korea and Japan, people used to worship the sun, and, like a living spirit, it would show up in birth dreams.

29

The sun is radiant and warm. Your child will be a great-hearted leader.

The mother of the Japanese Hideyoshi Toyotomi (born 1542), the "Great Conqueror of the Barbarians," dreamt that the Chinese character for the word "this" (*kore* in Japanese), appeared before her in the sky. The character can be broken down into elements meaning "Good Luck" and "Sun."

(Source: Mr. Nobohiro Shinji, professor from Japan)

Her son, Hideyoshi, born after this dream, was a bright, talented and lucky man who by uniting the warring states of Japan, became the most powerful person in the country. Later his luck changed when his fleet was destroyed in battles to invade Korea in 1592.

The following are contemporary Korean dreams:

I

In a dream, while my mother was weeding in a dry rice field, a large red spirit, like a sun in the sky, fell down into her skirt. The spirit cast such a strong light that she almost could not open her eyes.

My brother was born.

(Miss Chang, student)

A boy is found in a "dry" *yang* place. He gives off a "strong" inspiring "light."

2

In a dream, my mother got lost in a field of reeds while going on a picnic. She tried to find her way to her friends. The harder she tried, the more difficult it was. The field seemed to go on forever.

Presently the sun was setting. She was exhausted. The moment she lay down to sleep, she heard a baby crying. Opening her eyes, she saw it in the reeds. Nobody else was around it.

My elder sister was born. She is womanly, talented, but weak.

(Anon., student)

A girl is discovered in a fertile, wet place, "reeds."

This dream conjures up the story of the baby Moses, who was also found among the reeds, in *Exodus.*

Of my collected Korean dreams of the sun (See chart in Part Six.) 79% are for boys (男).

MOON

In early Korea, it was believed that the Harvest moon was a spirit, and could fertilize a woman's womb. Virgins, in flowing white dresses, danced in spirals, singing *Kanggang suwollae* under the full moon light, imitating the phases of the moon, hoping to be blessed with a child (According to legend, *Kanggang suwollae* also warned that "Barbarians—i.e., the Japanese—are coming hither across the waters"). Even now such a moon dance goes on in a young bride's dreams.

I

My mother said, "I was walking through a forest rich with many kinds of wild flowers and plants. The moon was shining very brightly.

While strolling across fields, I felt lonely. The moon became brighter and brighter, approaching me. I was gazing at it with wide open eyes, without any thought.

Suddenly some people came out of the moon, surrounded it, and they began to dance, holding hands in a circle. While I was absorbed in watching them, a cute little girl came running to me. Hugging the girl, I woke up."

A few months later, a cheerful girl was born.

She, my sister, is now married and has two children.

(Anon., teacher)

"Wild flowers" set the fertile *yin* mood for a girl. One in a dream is one in life, too.

2

Nicheren (1222–1282) was a Japanese Buddhist, who like a messiah, preached salvation to the common people of Japan. He founded the Nicheren sect.

Before his birth his mother dreamt that the sun and moon came down from the sky and floated into her mouth.

(Mr. Nobohiro Shinji, professor)

Her child would shine day and night.

Compare this Korean dream :

On May 23, 1936, I stood in the middle of a mountain. It was night. There was no wind and it was very dark. I was trembling.

The moon appeared in the sky. I could see many stars.

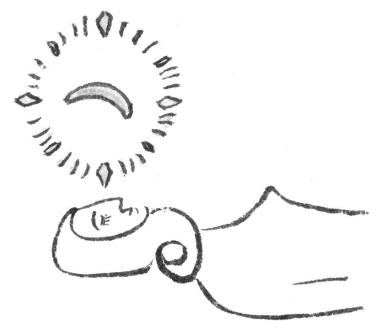

The moon glows. Your deep-hearted baby will gently lighten up the world.

It grew bright around me and my fears disappeared. I gazed at the moon for a long time.

Seeing the moon, I felt calm and comfortable. Suddenly it came up to me. I opened my mouth and ate it.

On January 8, 1937, I had a baby girl. She was cool, aggressive and persevering. She is now a Buddhist nun, and has her own temple on Ch'iak Mountain.

(Anon., teacher)

As a nun, she is free of sexual distinctions, and personifies the "calm and comfortable" brightness symbolized by the moon.

3

The bedroom window on the east side of our house faced the moon. The moonlight was reaching into my body, and I said. "It's hot."

The bedroom was full of light.

I gave birth to a boy. He is an architect.

(Woman met on a farm)

"East," is the direction of rising light. "Hot" is also *yang*, for a boy.

Moon dreams: 57% (男).

STAR

In ancient China, stars were thought of as spirits which, occasionally descended from Heaven like meteors, and gave life to exalted human beings.

The Chinese emperor Shao-hao (who reigned 2595 B.C.- ?) was regarded as the son of a star god. Donald Mackenzie in *Myths of China and Japan* says that, "One night his mother beheld a star, which resembled a rainbow, floating on a stream in the direction of a small island. After retiring to rest she dreamed that she received the star, and, in due course gave birth to her son."

For Koreans, the most famous star dreams concern General Kim Yu-shin, who, aided by T'ang China, was the hero of the Shilla kingdom's defeat of the kingdom of Paekche in 660 A.D., which led to the unification of the peninsula: One spring night, a magistrate was up late reading a book. In the dark sky, numerous tiny stars were twinkling, and the full moon was hanging above. Then he fell asleep and dreamed that while striding leisurely through a forest, looking up at the sky, he was astonished to see a huge, bright star rushing towards him. He tried to run away, but in vain. At last the star plunged into his breast, and he woke up afraid.

He realized it was not a mere dream. It was so vivid and shocking that he asked, "What on earth does it mean?" He thought about it over and over until dawn. During breakfast he told his wife about the dream, and was surprised to hear she too had been dreaming that she was walking along the garden in the night. A big, brilliant star appeared in the sky. After that, three of the surrounding stars drew near to the big star, bowing to it. The big star suddenly emitted a splendid light, rushing down to her. She held it by her breast, and fascinated, woke up.

When at last the baby was born, on his back were seven birth marks describing the Seven Stars of the Big Dipper.
(Mr. Cho, student)

"Three stars bowing down to one star," stood for the kingdoms of Shilla, Paekche and Koguryŏ bowing down to the one authority Kim Yu-shin represented.

One is struck here by the similarity to the dream of Joseph, in

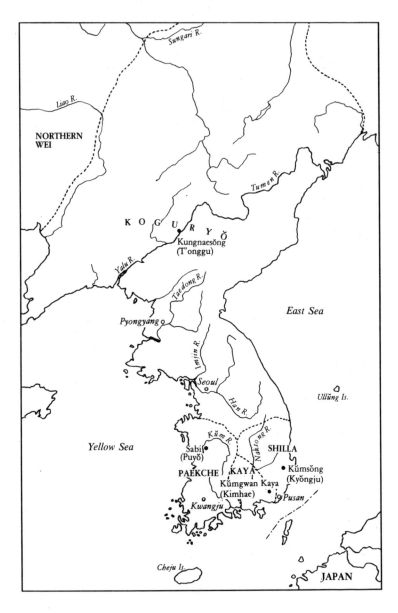

THE THREE KINGDOMS AND KAYA (ca. 600)

Genesis 37: 9. "...the sun and the moon and the eleven stars bowed down to me." The sun and moon meant Joseph's father and mother, and the eleven stars, his brothers, all of whom would fulfill his dream's prophecy. Even today in Korea, a shooting star stands for a brilliant leader.

1

Upon sighting a very big tiger, my mother couldn't help stopping and admiring its clear color, yellow and black stripes, and twinkling eyes. Opening its mouth wide, it cried out, and ate stars from the sky.

My mother approached, but it didn't roar anymore, and was polite to her.

After this, my elder brother was born. My grandfather-in-law named him "Ho-sŏng." *Ho* means "Tiger" and *Sŏng* means "Brave." Growing up, he was straight and brave. He is a lieutenant colonel in the Army.

(Anon., teacher)

A "very big" animal manifests the *yang* power of a boy.

2

My mother said, "One evening, I was plodding along a strange street. Moon and stars lit the dark sky.

Suddenly two girls approached. They looked very young, and said to me, "Follow us." So I followed, play-ing with them.

After playing, they gave me a little twinkling star. I was very happy and came back home smiling."

I, her daughter, am shy and silent. I teach primary school.

(Anon., teacher)

"Girls" give a daughter. A girl is also "little," which is *yin*. She will cast a small endearing *yin* light on the world.

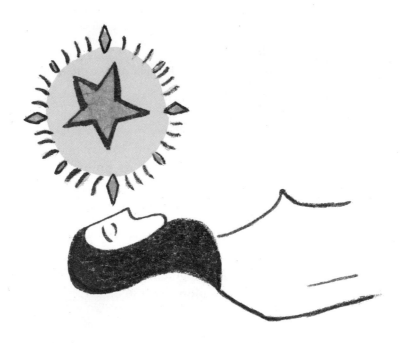

A star is warm and brilliant. Your bright-eyed baby will lead others as a general, or be a star on the stage.

3

My wife dreamed she climbed up a hill near our home-town. She liked being alone in the night air, staring up in wonder at the thousands of stars.

As she stood on top, the wind's touch was soft and she felt no fear. Suddenly a large star fell on her arm, and the wind raised her slowly from the earth. She was carried away, and soon lowered to rest on soft grass.

The sweet smell of flowers and the merry sound of a nearby brook made her feel that she was not alone. Closing her eyes, she was soon fast asleep.

Waking up, she found herself resting in our room.

Soon she became pregnant, and ten months later a boy was born. We call him "Han Pyŏl." *Han* means "Great;" *Pyŏl*, "Star." He is nine months old.

(Anon., teacher)

A boy is "large."
He will shine a guiding light over this world.
In Korea, a child is already regarded as being one month old upon conception.

4

My mother was looking out the window at many stars in the sky. Soon they entered her room through the window, falling on the floor. She could hear the sound of stars clattering down.

She looked in the mirror and found she was in a pink dress.

A son was born. As he grew older, he became gentle and ambitious. He is my brother, a freshman at Seoul National University, and studies applied arts.

(Miss Che, teacher)

A "pink dress" symbolizes maternity and a "gentle" child.
"So many stars clattering" mean an "ambitious" boy, because *yang* makes a lot of noise.

5

My wife told me, she was running over a bridge, and fell down (The river, due to rain, was flowing over the bridge).

Suddenly she saw a big, five-pointed star in the water. It was yellow and brilliant. She had never seen such a radiant star before.

Our child was a boy. He is seven months old now, very healthy and only cries when hungry.

(Anon., teacher)

The bridge spans a perilous river of life, which the child must cross; it may also be a phallic symbol.
"Big, radiant" and odd numbers are *yang* and so tell of a boy.
Star dreams: 66% 男.

METEOROLOGICAL SIGNS

For Orientals, the weather showed the pleasure or displeasure of "Heaven." It was its way of communicating with people on earth. Stormy or balmy messages were aimed at both awake and sleeping souls. If a person's conduct was in accord with the "will of Heaven" then she or he would receive an auspicious dream. A clear, dry, sunshiny atmosphere is *yang* and commonly meant a boy; and a cloudy, wet one, sometimes with a rainbow, is *yin*, a girl.

Min-bi, the last queen of the Yi dynasty, was brutally murdered on October 8, 1895 by Japanese agents, because she was felt to be an obstacle to their country's expanding influence over the affairs of Korea.
Her birth was presaged by her father, who dreamt of seeing a scarlet cloud in the sky above his house.
Coincidentally I had a dream of a scarlet cloud when I was pregnant with my first daughter.
(Mrs. Kwon, teacher)

Scarlet is a noble, though temperamental color.

THUNDER AND LIGHTNING

One Reverend Han, a Korean minister, said, "When

40

lightning hits someone in a birth dream, as it did my mother, it feels like being struck by an Atomic Bomb!"

"I was walking alongside an old castle. Suddenly there was thunder and lightning in the blue sky. Surprised, I fled back home."

My grandmother told the story to everybody she met. One day, an old neighbor woman, who had had many different kinds of experiences, told her, "It is a very nice dream if you have a boy. Because he will grow up into an honorable man. But if you have a girl, she will have a hard life."

My grandparents prayed to God for help, wishing to have a son. But my grandmother had my mother. They were disappointed because the baby was a daughter, but they took good care of her. She has been living happily.

(Miss Kim, student)

Perhaps the "old castle" was a new girl's wondrous womb; any kind of closed-in habitation is *yin*.

RAINBOW

My mother dreamt one winter day, it began to pour suddenly. The thunder rolled and rumbled, and lightning flashed for approximately three hours. My mother was left alone at home, and very frightened. She prayed for my father to come back as soon as possible.

Suddenly it stopped raining, and a shiny rainbow appeared through a high, clear sky. There was something mysterious about that rainbow, for it began in the sky, and finished on the roof of my house. My mother felt very happy. Then she was roused from a sound sleep.

I was the baby. My mother says that I will be an

important woman, for a rainbow means success and happiness.
(Miss Yun, student)

"A rainbow" shows off a heavenly girl.

SNOW

It was noon on a spring day. The sun was shining brightly. My aunt was doing some housework in the yard. Suddenly it began snowing in the sunshine.

Soon the snow changed into a snowball, and the snowball changed again into the form of a baby boy, drifting down to my aunt.

As soon as she received it in her arms, it melted into water, and the water was absorbed by her palms. She was so frightened, she lost her senses.

She had scarcely awakened when she told her husband the whole story. After about four months she bore a son. She told the dream to everyone she met.
(Mr. Pak, student)

A dream boy becomes a real one. Also, "snowing in the sunshine" is a glowing *yang* boy's atmosphere.

TERRESTRIAL SIGNS

WATER

One night, Mun-hŭi, the younger sister of the Shilla hero Kim Yu-shin (See star dreams), was listening to the story of a dream her older sister, Po-hŭi, had just had. Po-hŭi told her, "I was taking a walk and climbed up T'oham Mountain (above the capital city of Kyŏngju).

Lifting up my skirts, I began urinating on the top of the mountain. A lot of urine flowed down the mountain like a river, at last flooding the whole town."

Mun-hŭi thought it a lucky dream, and offered to buy it from her for a few feet of silk. Po-hŭi, who was afraid of the dream, agreed, and its power was given to her sister.

Later, Mun-hŭi married Kim Ch'un-ch'u, the heir to the Shilla throne (King Muyŏl, 654–661). She became Queen of Shilla, and the mother of royal children, instead of her sister, Po-hŭi, all because of buying the dream.

(Mr. Kim Young-jo, professor)

According to Lee Kyu-dong, M.D., in "Psychological Studies of T'aemong", Korean women used to climb up mountain tops to urinate en masse in order to evoke the response of "the great (male) god" in Heaven to send down rain, "sperm," in times of drought. The climbing itself, he said, was "a psychological orgasm."

Urinating on the mountain meant sending down new life waters to the capital city, as Mun-hŭi did, bearing royal children after she became queen.

Last night, as a result of writing the above passages, I, myself, had a dream:

I was on a small tropical island, surrounded by water. A typhoon blew up. On one side of the island, palm trees were bending down and the waves were rising. They were rising exceedingly high and I ran to the far, higher side of the island, up a cliff. But the tidal waves rose, threatening to engulf me.

Under the shadow of a looming wave, I hurried to the center of the island, up on a hill, where I found my wife sitting quietly in a room of a house. "You can stay here with me," she said. But I replied, "I'll look around a little, and come back."

The flood of waves was wiping out my old life on the island of my world and establishing a new relationship with my wife. Last night, she helped me translate an article on birth dreams and I felt a harmonious change in our feelings towards each other.

If Po-hŭi's "urination dream" can so affect my own dreams, and inspire me to change my life, so much more must it be able to affect a Korean's dreams.

The lady who lives next door told me, "After journeying on foot from sunrise till nearly noon on a summer's day, my weariness in the increasing heat decided me to sit down in the first convenient shade and await the coming of a vehicle.

As if specially for me, there soon appeared a little mass of trees with a delightful recess in their midst, and a fresh, bubbling spring, that seemed never to have sparkled for anyone but me. I knelt down by the spring and drank deeply of the fresh water. The taste of the water was sweet and delicate. Then I lay on the soft earth."

When she woke she guessed the water intimated a son. But she gave birth to a daughter.

(Miss Na, student)

Her guess should have been correct because *yang* water bubbles up and *yin* flows down.

ICE

In front of my gate were two big blocks of very clear ice (like those at a fish market). Between the ice blocks was an arching rainbow.

The sky held many stars, almost like sparkling flowers.

I had a daughter. She's a student.

(Woman met at a temple)

A "rainbow" bears an artistic, wide-ranging girl. Stars "like flowers" are also feminine.

44

"Ice" makes her cool, though of clear mind.

TREE

This is the story of I In (born in 1736 B.C.), a prime minister during the Shang dynasty in China. He was famous for initiating many reforms for the welfare of the people:

One day a young girl was carrying a basket in the forest and gathering mulberry leaves to feed her silk worms. Suddenly she heard the sound of a baby crying. She traced the sound to a mulberry tree and found a red

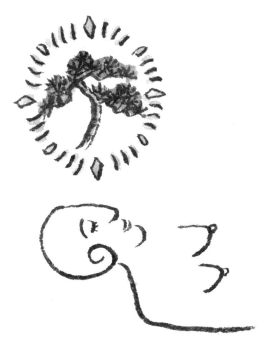

A pine tree has long life. Your baby will be a hardy sage.

45

baby crying inside the hollow trunk. The girl brought the baby to the king, and he ordered that the child be raised by the royal cook. Meanwhile, the king sent a man to verify the story about the baby.

Somebody said that the baby's mother was living by the bank of the I river. The king's man went there and learned from a villager that the woman had been pregnant, and that she dreamed that a god told her, "...when water begins to come out of the pestle (in which she pounded rice), go to the east and never look back." The next day, water came out of the stone pestle. The woman told her neighbor this story and set out for the east. Though her neighbor thought the story nonsense, a young mulberry leaf gatherer, who also heard it, was curious and followed after the dreamer.

After the pregnant woman had walked about ten kilometers she began to worry about her home and turned back. Returning, she found her house covered over by a flood and the water rose up after her. Miraculously, as the waves were lapping at her feet, she was metamorphosed into a mulberry tree, standing in the midst of the water.

A few days later, the mulberry leaf gatherer found the mulberry tree and the red baby cradled in it.

(Mr. Chang Shao-wen, professor from Taiwan)

Red was an auspicious color representing the sun and the south, a place of prosperity.

The story is reminiscent of Lot's wife, in *Genesis*, who, looking back at her old home, was changed into a pillar of salt.

The dream for the birth of the ideal teacher and student of social morals, Confucius (551–479 B.C.), seems related to the above story:

Cheng-tsai was walking by a lake (another account says on a mountain) and fell asleep on a grave-mound. While sleeping she dreamt of making love with a mysterious Black Emperor, who told her, "You will give birth to a child inside a mulberry tree."
She awoke and fourteen months later, gave birth to Confucius inside the trunk of a hollow mulberry. He is called the "First Sage," because mulberry bark is used for making writing paper.
(Mrs. Wang Su-yi, professor from Taiwan)

The following Korean dream seems to be a synthesis of the above Chinese stories:

On the morning of October 20, 1982, my husband said to me, "I had a very strange dream..."
There was a very old and tall ginkgo tree near his childhood house. This ginkgo had a big hole in it. When my husband walked near the tree, he saw a girl sitting in the big hole and crying.
She was very pretty. So he carried her home in his arms.
We had a girl on April 15, 1983. She is a lively child.
(Mrs. Ch'oe, teacher)

A girl in a dream is one in life. She is inside, *yin*.

FIRE

I

One day, in a dream, while my mother was wandering on a mountain, an old man with long white hair, called a "mountain god," appeared. He wore white clothes and carried a stick.

47

He commanded her, "Make a deep bow toward this...
bow!" She looked up to where he was pointing. There was
an enormous thorny thicket. Surprised, she bowed and
bowed and bowed....

After a while she knew that her husband had come, and
they bowed together, bowed and bowed.... They raised
their heads to look up, and how wondrous it was! The
thicket had caught on fire and was burning briskly.
Flames were rising up in the air.

I, a boy, was born four months later.

Mother thought this dream lucky. I am doing my best
to please her.

(Mr. Yang, student)

A boy's creative *yang* flames "up."
One is reminded of the wonder of Moses and the burning bush in
Exodus.

2

My mother told me, "In late fall, the mountain was
covered with falling leaves and bare trees. I and a few
other women were harvesting rice in a golden field below.
Suddenly we saw a fire flaring in the nearby mountains.
In a few moments, the streak of fire began growing
towards the village. Curiously our house was not
damaged, though the neighboring houses were practically
all burnt out."

My elder brother was born. My mother sees the dream
as God's luck, because fire means prosperity, and the
survival from loss means endurance in the face of adversity.

(Mr. Pak, student)

Here, the *yang* prosperity of a son, "flaring fire," is gained at the
expense of neighbors.

Mountains live long and are tranquil. Your baby will be a strong and steady worker.

MOUNTAIN

My mother dreamed she picked up a tall mountain, turning it upside-down. It trembled and she swallowed it from the top, like a horn.
Afterwards I was born. Now I live on a mountain.
(Monk at Haein Temple, Kaya Mt.)

A boy has "a horn," which is *yang*.
When grown up, his "spirit" again embodied a mountain.

Part Two

DREAM GARDENS

Gardens of Earth abound with life. A woman watches seeds sprouting in the furrows. She sees flowers and vari-colored fruits and vegetables appearing, each in its season. She relates to them and their memories flood her dreams when it is time for her to bear fruit, too.

"About the year 670 B.C., a concubine of count Wen of Cheng had a dream. A messenger from Heaven appeared to her, and handed her an orchis plant. The concubine became enceinte, and gave birth to a male child, who was named Lan, Orchis, and became the count Mu of Cheng. Later, count Mu having fallen ill, said, 'As long as the orchis lives, I will not die, because its life is mine....' Someone having destroyed the orchis, the count died, in 606."

(Leo Wieger, *A History of Religious Beliefs...in China)*

FlOWERS

Chŏng Mong-ju (1337–1392 A.D.) was an influential Neo-Confucian scholar and court official. A virtuous person, due to his loyalty to the last king of Koryŏ, he was assassinated (beaten to death with a hammer) by a conspiring son of Yi Sŏng-gye. Yi, the child of a golden yardstick dream, then, usurped the throne and established his own Yi dynasty of Chosŏn (1392–1910).

One morning, upon awakening, Chŏng's mother looked

over at her husband and said, "I dreamed a very strange dream."

"Strange dream? Please tell me about it."

"I'm afraid to."

"Hurry up! Tell me!"

"I had a flowerpot of orchids in my arms and dropped it on the ground."

"What? A flowerpot of orchids?"

"Yes. The flowerpot was shattered, but the orchids were not spoiled."

"Ha-ha! Ha-ha!"

"I can't stand it. Why are you laughing?"

"I can't help it. You had a good dream."

"Why?"

"It's a birth dream."

"Is it?"

"Orchids are very noble flowers. The flowerpot was broken, but the orchids were not spoiled. This means the baby who's going to be born will be very noble."

Chŏng Mong-ju was born that very year. The *Mong* in his name means "Dream."

(Mr. Yi, student)

The flowers represented his spirit, which lives on as an example of loyalty for the Korean people. The pot was his broken skull.

UNNAMED FLOWERS

I

One summer day, my mother was walking along the Tŏksu Palace stone wall. She was beautiful as an angel and happy.

Many flowers, especially roses, bloomed all over. A butterfly flew from one flower to another. The sun was gentle. My mother talked with many flowers, and continued walking.

A flower opened in her footprint as she stepped forward. A succession of flowers bloomed in each footprint. At last she was buried under many flowers, and awoke. Ten months later, she bore me. I am a kind woman. (Anon., teacher)

Flowers, like girls, are soft, colorful and pretty.
Flowers are the most common dreams for girls(女). 84% are 女.

2

My uncle saw a big white flower in the center of a field. It was fall. The rice was doing well, tossing in the vast field. He went into the field to pick the flower. He could see it clearly, but could not find the way to it.

Going around here and there, he picked up a chestnut and three persimmons. After picking, he stretched out on his back. Just then he found the flower by his nose. He plucked it and was trying to put it into his pocket. Doing so, he woke up....

My aunt had a daughter. She's a student. (Anon., teacher)

ASSORTED FLOWERS

I

Arm in arm,
my mother and father
searched a cavern
and found a gold-lit pond.

Lots of lotuses
were covering it,
dewdrops

on curling leaves.

*I, a light-
hearted girl,
was born.*

(Anon., teacher)

2

On a foggy day, my mother was walking along a narrow path when she smelled a wondrous fragrance. She kept on in its direction and found a heavenly sight in front of her: a pavilion on a placid lake full of lotus blossoms.

A lotus is beautiful and serene. Your child will be lovely, meditative.

In the small temple was a pretty little girl studying a strip of calligraphy. "Oh, this is paradise!," my mother thought.

While she was watching these sights, one of the water-flowers which were strewn over the lake flashed out into her breast.

She got pregnant just after this dream.

I, a girl, came into this world. According to the dream, I was supposed to be a precocious, well-mannered lady, and pretty like a lotus blossom. I also ought to be studying like the girl, and that's who I am.

(Miss Cho, student)

3

There was a large pond of dirty water. In the pond, a white lily was in bloom. It was so big that it filled up the pond without any gaps. It was such a bright white that no one could look straight at it. There were other flowers, but they could not be compared with its size and beauty.

My mother was flying and singing as if she were an angel. The sky was clear. The sun threw a light on her face.

After that, my sister came into this world. Beautiful and kind-hearted, she is studying to become a missionary.

(Miss Cho, student)

4

The stars were shining brightly and descending to the mother-to-be. She smiled and shook her head unconsciously. There were various colored roses around the stars. They were white, green, yellow, and red.

Some stars handed red roses to her. She accepted and appreciated them. She kept the red roses and was walking along the street, loving their sweet scent.

While she was walking along carelessly, she stumbled, and began an endless fall. It seemed that she was approaching death, and she nearly fainted. But, suddenly, she felt the roses were fluttering up like big birds to save her. So she was finally able to land on a safe place with the help of the roses. When she looked for the stars, they had already disappeared.

She awoke, and thought it a wonderful dream.

Soon her child was born. It was a pretty girl. The girl always looked at stars hopefully and raised various kinds of roses.

As her mother loved the stars in the sky, so her daugh-

A rose has a heart of love. Your baby will be beautiful, and compassionate.

58

ter wanted to become a star in a play. She wanted to become an actress who was loved by everyone. After all she became an actress and everybody called her "Star." Now, as everyone wants to see the stars at night, so everyone wants to see her in a play.

Her mother constantly reminds her of her relationship with the stars, and she loves them because they had saved her mother from a dangerous fall.

(Miss Pang, student)

5

In her mother's dream, a hill was covered with azaleas. A stream ran merrily in front of the hill, and two Buddhist nuns were gathering flowers nearby. They were grumbling over something, and were carrying knapsacks on their backs.

Mrs. Kim, an old lady who lives in our neighborhood, was born just after this. She had two sons, but they both died young; and her husband was a playboy. She began to cry telling me this story, and said, "The knapsacks must mean adversity."

(Mrs. Lee, teacher)

Azaleas, as in Kim So-wol's famous poem, *Azaleas,* signify a lost love.

ARTIFICIAL FLOWERS

There were many artificial flowers in a basket. I put it on my head, and many other people beside me put such baskets on their heads.

I fell down on the ground with the flowers, by accident. Picking the basket up again, I saw that they weren't ruined.

The life of those flowers was forever. They wouldn't wilt, and foretold a son who could keep the bloodline.

I gave birth to a son. He is four years old, and doesn't give up trying to get whatever he wants.

(Mrs. Pak, teacher)

A boy is dry, and carried high on the head for all to see.

FRUITS

Maybe this was Eden. My mother was walking about in fresh air and very bright sunshine. She crossed a stream so transparent that she could see through to the dancing of fish. There were many trees. Some were fragrant, so she could think only of beautiful things. And some had very sweet fruits. Picking two, she put them in her pocket. Even though this seemed like Heaven, the most comfortable place for her was home.

She returned home and took the beautiful fruits out of her pocket. Do you know what happened? They had turned into ugly blue ones. Though disappointed, she kept them.

On my mother's birthday, she gave birth to my younger brother.

(Miss Kim, student)

"Beautiful" red fruit, like ladies dressed in traditional Korean dresses, as I suppose these to have been before they changed, would likely have given her a girl.

Blue is more becoming of a Korean man's customary clothes, thus a boy was born.

APPLE

One day, my mother ascended a small hill to pick some wild, edible greens with her friends. There was a rainbow and birds sang in the sky. There were many apple trees around. She and her friends rejoiced as if they had entered a wonderland. Suddenly my mother had a desire to eat apples, but her friends had no such interest. Therefore, they went off, picking greens in another place. But my mother stayed behind picking apples instead.

After a while, her friends returned. They found my mother's bamboo basket was filled with many apples. So

An apple is round and juicy. Your jolly child will have many children.

61

they asked, "Why did you pick only apples and no greens?" My mother didn't even answer them. As a result, her friends went on down a small hill. Though my mother remained alone, she picked more and more apples. However, she couldn't eat but one, because she devoted herself to picking. Then the apples' weight tore her skirt. Apples scattered on every side. As soon as she dropped down to pick them up, she stumbled over an apple.

She awoke from the dream, astonished.

My mother said the dream was for me.

(Miss Lee, student)

Apple dreams: 83% 女, the one she stumbled over became her's.

CHERRY

My aunt climbed a mountain, walking here and there without reason. During that time, she found a tree with three cherries on it. Only one was beautiful, so she picked it off.

She took it in her hand, continuing along a path and confronted a precipice. She peered down to the bottom, and surprisingly, many beautiful flowers were there.

After a few moments, she woke up.

Her daughter has a very quiet personality, and mostly plays in her room.

(Miss Pak, student)

Cherry dreams: 100% 女, because *yin* is small, round and red (in fruit) like a cherry.

"Flowers" decorate a girl.

GRAPE

There were many grapes in a vineyard. Under the

grape vines, a woman was standing alone. She alone was moving.

All of a sudden, the vines began to move and tried to swallow her. But it was not easy.

After a while, she ate the grapes greedily. As soon as she ate them, many horns appeared, growing from her body. She became a grape vine.

A son was born.

(Mrs. Kim, teacher)

A boy has a horn (thorn).
Grape dreams: 100% 男, because grapes resemble testicles.

MANGO

Traditionally, a market day was held every five days and there were various seed sacks in the stalls. My wife went out "window-shopping" with my sister-in-law.

Meanwhile, she spotted an old man selling various seeds on the street. She approached him, pointing at some red seeds. "What kind of seeds are those?," she asked.

He replied, "Those are mangoes."

Mangoes are not raised in our country, but my wife decided to grow them in our garden and bought lots of seeds. The old man included many extra seeds in the bargain. He threw a handful into her skirt, and she caught all of them.

She went back home, and planted them in our garden. She sprinkled water on the seeds and earnestly cultivated them. They flourished to bear mangoes. We divided these with my relatives and neighbors. They were pleased.

A few months later, my wife gave birth to a healthy boy. He is living in America now with his mother, and is seven months old. According to my wife, he is very

healthy and cheerful.
(Mr. Lee, teacher)

A long, hard seed, such as a mango's, is for a boy. Because of a foreign fruit, he was destined to grow up in a foreign land.

MELON

My mother saw a brightly shining brook. The water was very fresh and clean. She waded in, lifting up her skirt, and some beautiful fish swam around her. Catching sight of a glimmer in the water, she looked carefully, and found a big, yellow melon. Lifting it out, she ate it. It was delicious.

Five months later she had me, a daughter.
(Miss Kang, student)

A girl's *yin* sinks down.
"Big" is ripe, which means much cool water, or *yin* in fruit; and "yellow," is generous.

ORANGE

One night, while I was heading somewhere, a goat suddenly appeared and obstructed my way. So I chose a side road, and just then, with a strong wind, many big, attractive oranges fell down, rolling on the ground. I picked them up, filling up my skirt to my heart's content, and ate a few which had split open.

After the dream, I was pregnant and bore a girl.

I guess I had a girl because I had eaten the split oranges. She is a bit shrewd, a middle school student.
(Anon., teacher)

She rejected the goat's aggressive behavior in favor of the

oranges' passive, falling movement, and so bore a girl, "split."

PEACH

Wandering about a small village under the moonlight, I found a peach orchard. There was no guard, so I strolled on through under the peach trees until I felt thirsty.

I gathered ripe peaches in my skirt. When my skirt was full, I took one of them and ate it. It was the most delicious peach I'd ever tasted.

My child was a girl. She has a sharp temper, and is a housewife.

(Anon., teacher)

Girls are gathered under *yin* "moonlight," and are "ripe."

Peach dreams: 53% 女. A peach has both *yin* and *yang* characteristics: though its flesh is soft, sweet and juicy, its seed is big and hard.

PEAR

Roving
in the trees,

a golden pear
appeared on a stem
before my eyes.

I smiled slowly,
trying to grasp it
in my hand...

but it was made of pure light
floating through my body.

I bore
a gentle girl.

(Anon., housewife)

PERSIMMON

It was warm spring, but curiously, in a young woman's dream, it was autumn. All the trees were bare of leaves and the field and mountain were yellow, speckled with bits of green and red. A small stream was flowing beside the trees with ripe persimmons.

The young woman approached the trees. She put about fifteen fruits in her apron. She felt very happy and pleased going carefully home.

Entering her room, she put the basket down without eating the fruit.

After ten months, a girl was born. Her parents loved her especially, like the persimmons in the apron. In childhood, she studied Korean dancing and piano. She was playful and pretty.

She wants to live in nature, and her favorite season is autumn. She is growing silent gradually. Who is the girl? It's me.

(Miss Shin, student)

A girl was traditionally kept safely in a "room."

Persimmon dreams: 32% 女, because though persimmons may be juicy and sweet, or *yin*, they leave a dry aftertaste in the mouth, which is *yang*. Also, persimmon seeds are long and hard, or *yang*.

POMEGRANATE

My mother was at her father-in-law's house. She was in the field, picking many pomegranates. They were very ripe. Some had cracked open. Gathering them, she filled up her apron.

As she was turning to go back to the house, such a big sun was coming up in the sky. It was shining bright enough to hurt her eyes. She hid her eyes with her hand against the strong sunlight.

I was born.

(Mr. Ch'oe, teacher)

The "big sun shining bright" shows a son's vitality.
A pomegranate cracking open promises abundant children, or riches.

STRAWBERRY

My friend's mother found some very attractive, wild strawberries on a snow-covered grave. Picking off a few, she returned home.

A month passed and she became pregnant.

She said, "Strawberries mean a pretty, charming daughter. Snow means a white dress."

My friend is very kind, bright, and has a strong will. She is a white-clad nurse.

(Anon., teacher)

A "grave" suggests renewal of life.
Strawberry dreams: 100% 女, because of so many small, soft seeds of life.

WATERMELON

There were many kinds of flowers all over. My grandmother was fascinated by their beauty. She wanted all of them, but did not pick any.

When she was winding through the field of flowers, suddenly a big watermelon appeared in front of her. Very surprised, she fled away. Moments later she paused,

returning to it, recognizing that it was just a watermelon.
She looked at it for a long time, wanting to eat it, and
then split it open with a stone, gobbling it up in the
twinkling of an eye. Strangely enough there wasn't even
one black seed inside.
She had a full stomach and soon fell asleep in the field
of flowers.
She became pregnant with my mother.
(Miss Won, student)

A girl is found amidst "flowers."
A seedless fruit is *yin*, all water, a virgin. A "full stomach"
equals her mother's pregnancy.

NUTS

In 1949, my mother dreamt that she went gathering
nuts with three other women who lived in the same
village. Every woman found a rotten nut, except my
mother. She got a good one.
Afterwards, the women who had gone gathering nuts
began to conceive. Of course my mother conceived, too.
And each woman gave birth to a child.
The children of the three women who had found rotten
nuts died during the Korean War in 1950. But the child of
the woman who got a good nut survived. I am he.
(Mr. Yun, teacher)

How could such destinies be known even before conception?
One Oriental medical professor, Song Sa-myŏng, visiting Korea
from China, said, "Just as the 'Spirit of God' breathed life into
Adam in your Western *Bible*, so does the intuitive nature of a
woman receive the message of God through the bio-electricity of
her body, in her dreams "

ACORN

One day, my sister-in-law's friends gave her some Korean (rice) cakes. She was carrying them to eat at her house. But when she got home, they had changed into acorns.

According to the ultrasound examination in the hospital, a son will be born.

(Mrs. Kim, teacher)

An acorn, inside the shell, resembles a boy's penis.

CHESTNUT

During the Japanese Occupation of Korea (1910-1945), the patriotic Kim Ku organized anti-Japanese terrorist operations and a provisional Korean government from his base in Shanghai. Before Kim was born, in 1876, his mother dreamt that "she picked a red chestnut out from a blue chestnut burr."

To inspire him, she would occasionally remind him of the dream, for the colors resembled the red and blue, circular *T'aegŭk* symbol on the Korean flag.

(Sŏk Sŏng-u, *T'aegyo*)

In my father-in-law's dream, there was a chestnut tree in our front yard. In fact, we have no trees like that. Suddenly quite a number of nut burrs began falling, so that the ground was soon covered with them.

Calming himself down, he put them into a sack. Even though hit by the thorny burrs on his head and back, he felt no pain.

Then he saw one of the fallen burrs had split into two

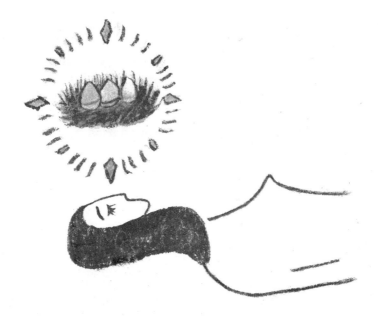

Chestnuts are soft inside, but prickly outside. Your baby's body guards a tender heart.

pieces, all by itself, and rays of light were streaming out of it. The nuts were all wine-colored and sleek as a cat, and plump as a baby's cheeks.

They began merging together into a bigger nut in the brightness. When the brightness broke away, there remained only this nut.

I had a daughter.

(Anon., teacher)

A girl yields to the force of gravity. She is "split," ready to receive, or here, emit *yang* light.

Chestnut dreams: 50% 女. Chestnuts are soft inside, easily decayed or *yin*; but also have hard, *yang*, outer husks and shells.

70

WALNUT

I was married in October, 1981. Shortly after the wedding ceremony, my wife and I took a honeymoon trip to Cheju Island. That night I dreamed it was a very beautiful day and I was sitting alone on a bench in my house. The sky was blue and clear. The sun was bright and warm. Suddenly I heard my name being called three times. I didn't answer because the voice wasn't familiar to me. But when I looked around I saw an old man with long, white hair and a beard coming toward me.

At first, I didn't recognize him. But when he drew near I found that it was my father, who had died in 1972. He was dressed in white. I was very happy to see him again, so I shouted, "Father!" But he said nothing to me. I was frustrated.

After a while, he took something out of his pocket and handed it to me. It was two walnuts. Then he left without a word. I tried breaking one of them open to eat it. But I couldn't, because it suddenly became golden. The two walnuts were shining very brightly. I thought them strange.

Soon my wife came back from the supermarket. I told her the story and gave her the walnuts. She took them gladly, putting them in her purse.

Just then I awoke and found that I was in my bed in the hotel. My wife was still sleeping. It was a beautiful morning.

The next year, my wife gave birth to a baby boy. He is a reserved, good-natured four year old child. Though very young, he can learn things very fast. He has memorized sixty short storybooks for children.

(Mr. Sŏng, teacher)

Father's "spirit" wished to give a son to preserve the family line.
"Walnuts" resemble testicles, and this is why about 86% of walnut dreams are 男.

"Golden" confers intelligence, which a brain-shaped nut suggests.

VEGETABLES

CUCUMBER

The monk Tosŏn (827–898) traveled all over the kingdom of Shilla. locating sites for temples, using the

*A cucumber is cool, but sensual. Your child may be plain
in appearance, but very fertile.*

72

Oriental art of geomancy. When his mother was a young bride, she dreamt that she ate a big cucumber. When a woman eats a large vegetable shaped like a male organ she is likely to have a son.
(Ch'a, Chŏng, and Lee, "Boy Preference")

I, my younger sister and sister-in-law were looking for cucumbers in the field. My sister-in-law passed the other two women by, going on ahead and pinched off two small cucumbers.

I sought some cucumbers of my own. To my surprise, I found a long, strong one. I said to my sister-in-law, "Why did you miss it, and pick such small ones?"

My sister-in-law has two daughters, and I have a son.
(Mrs. Pak, teacher)

Maybe she picked "small," *yin* ones because she preferred girls.

EGGPLANT

When my mother was about twenty years old, she dreamed that she plucked three eggplants from a vegetable garden, and then gave them to her elder brother's wife (who was eighteen years old), after taking a bite out of one of them.

She had a strange feeling because she thought that this was a birth dream, but she was not married. She phoned her sister-in-law to ask her if she was pregnant (she was living in a different city). Oddly enough, she answered, "Yes."

She gave birth to triplets (boys). But one of them is handicapped. All are thirteen years old.
(Miss Min, student)

Eggplants are phallic. The "bite" crippled one.

GARLIC

My grandmother was picnicking on Pugak Mountain.
She began looking for a drink. Fortunately, she found a
mineral spring and relieved her thirst.
Cloves of garlic were spread out, floating in the water.
Putting them into her skirt, she headed home.
She had my uncle.
(Miss Kang, student)

A boy floats above.
Garlic is an energetic root, and usually means a boy, still one
dream of a woman hiding a bunch behind a picture frame told of
a secretive girl.

GINSENG

I

My sister was climbing Ha Mountain (near my home-
town), which is famous for several interesting myths. At
the top, she found a huge ginseng root. There were a lot
of people surrounding her, who tried to snatch it away.
However, she couldn't run away from them, couldn't even
move her feet. She searched for her husband among those
people, but it was difficult to find him. Finally he was
there, but he looked too small and weak to eat it.
Running just a little away, they divided it into two
parts, and each of them swallowed one. She thought that
it was very easy to eat and that it was not a ginseng, but
a child.
Just after the dream, she conceived. A baby boy was
born. She had thought it would be a boy, because while in

74

her womb he had moved very energetically. He has a hot temper. He moves very fast and roughly, can speak difficult words and sentences beyond his age, and has a good imagination.
(Mrs. Chŏn, teacher)

A coveted boy is "huge." From a folk point of view, many "spirits" can invade one's dream; here, jealous ones.
Ginseng dreams: 82% 男, since roots are stimulating, or *yang*.

2

I was walking in a thick forest by my father's tomb, but I was not afraid of being alone. As soon as I touched the tomb, I was surprised by a large fountain springing forth from it. I had the feeling it was composed of my father's tears and I began to cry, falling down.

Time elasped, and all of a sudden I raised my head and began digging up his tomb as if he had been calling me from inside. Then I grasped something—it was a wild ginseng as big as a child. I put it in my skirt. Up until that time the fountain had continued to spring up and made a wonderful rainbow. I lost my senses for a while; a drop of water hit me, and I suddenly woke up.

Eight months later I had a girl. She is mild and steady.
(Mrs. Yŏm, teacher)

A "wonderful rainbow" personifies a wondrous girl.
Some ginseng roots are advertised as having sensuous, feminine "legs."

GOURD

There was a tidy, country house surrounded by many trees. Oddly, the tearful voices of frogs in front of the

75

stream suddenly stopped. A gourd in the bright moonlight lay solitary on a grass roof, just like another full moon and so ripe it seemed it would break.

In the deep night, my mother was surprised at the sudden cessation of the frogs crying, and shrouded by a strange feeling she went out into the yard. However, she was at a loss as to what to do in an ecstasy between the moon and the appetizing gourd on the roof.

She cut the trunk of the gourd, and it rolled down. She caught it, fortunately, in her arms, but decided to cut it in half, with a big saw, making a rasping sound, "sŭk-sak, sŭk-sak..."

A pretty rabbit ran out of the gourd, and jumped up and down with pleasure.

After several months, my mother gave birth to me, a girl. I was born in the Year of the pretty Rabbit. I study hard, love deeply and play away my time.

(Miss Ch'a, student)

A girl is "ripe" and moon-shaped, "cut in half," and "pretty."

In a folk tale, *Hŭngbu's Story*, three magical gourds containing treasures were cut open with a saw, which made the "sŭk-sak" sounds.

RED PEPPER

I saw an old man with a large bamboo basket. He came up and gave it to me. There were about a thousand red peppers in it.

I took them very gratefully, and then looked around for him to further express my thanks. But I couldn't find him. He had already left. I was very sorry.

Sitting on the rock, I began counting red peppers. "One, two, three,...fifty-five, fifty-six,..." Then I heard a noise.

A red pepper is long and hot. Your baby will be a fiery fighter, passionate lover.

My husband was waking me.

The child was a boy. He is friendly, idealistic, and honest. He is thirty years old, an electrical engineer.

(Mrs. Mok, teacher)

Pepper (mostly red) dreams: 68% 男. Because of a red pepper's suggestive shape and color, the Korean word for it, *koch'u*, means "penis."

POTATO

There was a dark cloud in late June. It was going to rain at any moment. It started: the rains of early summer.

In order to dig out some potatoes before they were spoiled, my mother hurried to the field. Arriving, she could see the yellowish potato leaves. A cool wind was passing through the field.

At first, she pulled on the leaves to bring up the potatoes. They were big, round and white. She unearthed as many as she could, putting them in her apron.

After she came back, she boiled them. Upon eating, she woke up.

I think my skin is extremely white and soft. It's because my mother ate so many sweet, white potatoes during that time. I am reserved, tolerant and a good girl.
(Miss Lee, student)

"Dark cloud" and "rain," "leaves" and earth tell of a modest girl.

Potato dreams: 78% 男, because potatoes are usually regarded as phallic.

PUMPKIN

"A few days after recognizing my first pregnancy, I dreamed of seeing my house. Its roof was matted with pumpkin vines. Then they bore two pumpkins. Also, the front yard was covered with pumpkin vines and seven pumpkins sprouted out.

While I was looking at them, a strange man entered my house. After he came back out, he picked off one of the pumpkins in the yard, and I was awakened."

These nine pumpkins represented my friend's mother's children; the two on the roof her sons, and the seven in the yard her daughters. She gave birth to seven daughters, but one died early. The strange man was a messenger from the "other world."

All the children have similar characters. The oldest son is engaged in journalism, and is introspective, but active. The younger son is a college student. Five of the six daughters are married; all are liberal and sociable.

(Miss Ko, student)

Boys sit on a high place; and girls. a low one.
Pumpkin dreams: 58% 男.

The "other world" is where we come from before being conceived in "this world," and also where we go after death.

After death, according to various Korean folk beliefs, which are a blend of shamanism, Taoism, Buddhism, and Christianity, we dissolve into airy and earthy elements, or journey to a subterranean world similar in landscape and population to our own, maybe below the grassy, womb-shaped Korean grave mounds, always able to come back in dreams upon calls of need from our loved ones, or else we exist as spirits in another airy dimension, perhaps on the other side of the sky, or "on the moon."

Before birth, either we haven't existed at all and are created anew from primal elements by the "Cosmic Spirit," or otherwise as bits of the "spirits" of the sun, moon and stars, and by gods like the Heaven and Dragon Kings, or else we are only reborn, returning from "the other world," along with seeds of plants and animals, through endless cycles of transmigrating souls.

RICE

My aunt told me, "It was a pitch dark night. I was walking along a gravelly place with an injured leg.

Suddenly a beam of light was shining brightly and shot into my mouth, I was dazzled.

After a while, there was a lunar eclipse. Just then I saw a stack of grain on the threshing ground of our home. It had no end, reaching up to the sky. The grain was golden yellow. It was a great spectacle.

Rice means harvest. Your child will always have enough to eat.

I gave easy birth to a boy. Composed and calm, he is an announcer for a broadcasting station in Masan. The grain means wealth."
(Mrs. Shin, teacher)

"A beam of light" eclipsing the moon and "grain up to the sky" manifest a dazzling boy.

SQUASH

I was passing through a field and found two squashes: twin green ones. Picking one up, I noticed its bottom was rotten.

The boy died three days after birth.
(Bus driver's mother-in-law)

A woman can innately learn of anything which is happening in her own body, though a dream.

SWEET POTATO

Before I tell you my mother's dream, I must explain about the customary Korean kitchen. It had lots of functions: besides cooking, family members could bathe there, and in the corner was a place where we could pile up bundles of hay for domestic animals.

Early one morning, Mother was working merrily, preparing breakfast. But strangely her eyes couldn't stop staring at the bundle of hay that was laying in the corner. She felt strongly that something must be in that bundle, so she put her hand in the hay and found a queer looking sweet potato. It was rather big, fatter than an ordinary one and looked very tasty.

As she was wondering how that sweet potato had gotten into the bundle, she woke up.

After a few days, she recognized she was pregnant. My brother is twenty four years old, tall and somewhat fat.
(Miss Kang, student)

"Rather big" indicates a healthy boy.

Part Three

DREAM ZOOS

Creatures of forests and streams bear their young, and sometimes an explorer will bring home a minnow, a fawn or even a tiger's cub to be raised by his family.

The barnyard, too, is full of the newly born: chicks, piglets, calves and foals, puppies and kittens, giving suggestions for a newly conceived woman's dreams.

"In a dream, I visited an eminent professor of Korean folklore to ask, "Where do birth dreams come from?" But as I was sitting on the sofa in his office I found out for myself; I saw a butterfly flitting through the office air. It was like a ghost butterfly, a transparent gray, and its big, rounded wings fluttered freely in the air.

Up in the corner of the room, near the ceiling, it disappeared, and appeared again, fluttering. Again, out of the empty gray air it appeared, a gray ghostly outline, vanishing in a flicker!

The professor had been out of the room for those moments. When he returned, I told him, "..." Mystified, he listened...

INSECTS

BEE

One day, my mother was busy washing my father's Army uniform. Suddenly a honey-bee flew down under her eyes. She tried feeding it some rice, but it quickly stung a sleeve of the uniform. Startled, she woke up. A few days later, she gave birth to my older brother. She guessed rightly that the boy would be a disciplinarian. He succeeded my father as an Army officer, and works like a bee!

(Mrs. Yi, teacher)

A boy may sting his father, because two *yangs* tend to clash; but a *yin* and a *yang* complement each other.

BUTTERFLY

Chuang-tzu was a third century Chinese, Taoist philosopher, a disciple of Lao-tzu. "Chuang-tzu was in the habit of sleeping during the day, and at night would transform himself into a butterfly, which fluttered gaily over the flowers in the garden. On waking, he would still feel the sensation of flying in his shoulders. On asking Lao-tzu the reason for this, he was told: 'Formerly you were a white butterfly which, having partaken of the quintessence of flowers and of the *yin* and the *yang*, should have been immortalized; but one day you stole some peaches and flowers in Wang-mu Niang-niang's garden. The guardian of the garden slew you, and that is how you came to be reincarnated.' At this time he was fifty years of age."

(E.T.C. Werner, *Dictionary of Chinese Mythology*)

In a sense this is how a birth dream works. The distinction between flesh and spirit is blurred in the Orient. A baby's "spirit" dreams that it is a butterfly and, while dreaming, encounters a woman, who catches it in her own dream. It wakes up as her child.

A contemporary Korean novelist, Lee Seung-hun says:

The dream is the most vivid in my memory of all the dreams I have ever dreamt. I thought that only women could have birth dreams. But I was wrong. *T'aegŭk* butterfly! I suppose that some people know what the *T'aegŭk* butterfly is. Nowadays, we can't hear this name. But it was often carried in the newspapers in the 1960's, "A Butterfly Found with *T'aegŭk* Designs on its Wings." And that *T'aegŭk* butterfly appeared to me in a dream. It was flying on a very beautiful hill, through groves of trees, as in Eden. Many animals were moving about on the hill: a cow, a horse, a pig, a hare, and so on. Oddly, the butterfly perched on the hare, although there were many other animals about.

In those days, we hadn't any children. I described this dream to my wife because it was marvelous to me.

She asked me, "Did the butterfly perch on the hare in your dream?"

"Yes, it did."

"Oh! What a lucky dream it is! Darling, you were born in the Year of the Rabbit, weren't you?"

"Yes, I was."

"Oh, that's a birth dream!"

"A birth dream?"

"Yes, it was a lucky dream because the *T'aegŭk* butterfly appeared."

"Can a man have a birth dream?"

"Of course! Well, let's see. We always regard the butterfly as a man and flowers as a woman, because a butterfly, as a rule, perches on a flower. Oh! A Son! I will surely bear a son!"

But she gave birth to a daughter. Her name is Kyu-yŏn. She grew up rapidly. Her personality is active, optimistic and cheerful. She is now a junior at a university.

(Reported by Mr. Kim, student)

In all fairness to Mr. Lee, this dream was really interpreted by his wife and not by him, and she was swept away by wishful emotions rather than having a sober regard for the dream.

Traditionally, in birth dreams, butterflies are daughters (about 86%), not sons. They are soft, dainty and low flying, or *yin*. They seem like little fairies wearing dresses. Only very big, bright specimens, such as tiger butterflies (See below), foretell boys.

Yet here the butterfly is very special, for being a *T'aegŭk* butterfly, it has both *yin* and *yang*, male and female characteristics in harmony, symbolizing the inter-play of nature as a whole, or creation; as does the symbol on the Korean flag. But the fact that it is a butterfly tends it to being a girl. Girls too are attracted to their fathers, if the hare indeed represents Mr. Lee.

Nevertheless, the *T'aegŭk* butterfly's blue and red commas on her wings make his daughter into a kind of angel of birth dreams, who flutters about the pages of this book, dispensing seeds of life to the world.

Two tiger butterflies were flitting in front of me. They were very big and I tried to shoo them away. But though I cried, "Go away!" three times, they didn't go away.

Instead, almost by accident, I caught one in my hand. When I woke up, my hand was still clasped.

After this I found I was pregnant, and bore a son.
(Mrs. Kim, housewife)

A boy is "very big," tigerish and disobedient, or *yang*.

Crying "Go away!" three times is a folk remedy for chasing away ghosts; Mrs. Kim recognized the butterflies were not ordinary.

MOTH

A pretty, yellow butterfly flew into my house. It was daytime and very hot.

Suddenly it changed into a black moth. I leaned over to crush it, but instead of killing it, I picked it up tenderly by

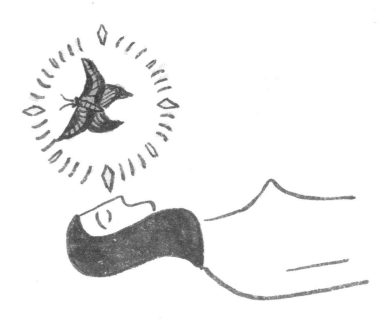

A dainty moth chases many lights. Your pretty child will dance and play through life.

its wings, so it could fly away outside.
My daughter is very pretty and healthy.
(Mrs. Pak, teacher)

The moth, being soft and small, and protectively dark, all *yin* qualities, is surely a girl.

FISH

"I dreamed,"
my wife told me
one morning,

"our long-tailed
red, white and gold
fish (who died)
came back;

swimming
around
and 'round

and through
my eyes."

"Funny, I dreamed
of them, too...," I replied.

(Y. I. and F. J. Seligson)

UNNAMED FISH

I

My mother met a poor widow. Her appearance was shabby and dirty. But her eyes were burning like stars. She begged for a meal. My mother prepared some food for her.

After finishing her dinner, she said to my mother, "Thank you for your kindness! You showed a little mercy to me. I would like to give you a gift. What do you want?"

"I want a baby," my mother answered.

"Oh, it's so easy to get a baby. Actually, I am a fortune-teller. Your wish will come true."

The fortuneteller's gift was a living fish. It was too hot to touch. But my mother could eat it without feeling any pain.

All of a sudden the poor woman disappeared in the air. And the hot fish became a baby in my mother's womb,

like a miracle.
After ten months a boy was born. It was me.
(Mr. Yi, student)

A boy is "hot."

2

My boarding-house keeper said, "I was walking alone
in a deep forest. From the top of a hill I saw a beach and
something was moving nearby. I could not see clearly
because of a thick mist.

Descending towards the beach and getting up close, I
could see a fish in the shallows between two rocks. It was
big with two small horns on its head. I caught it easily
and cradled it in my arms.

As I continued my walk, I happened to see a hut. Nobody was inside. I lay the strange fish down in the room
and peeped through a hole in the door. It changed into a
baby."

She explained that the dream means her son will be a
great person someday. He works for a company and has
a family.
(Mr. Lee, student)

"Big," and "horns" are signs of a boy's creative force.

3

My grandmother told me she had gone to the well to
fetch some water and saw a very big fish swimming
there. She reached in and caught it in her arms, but then
the fish jumped back in the well with my grandmother,
too! She woke up astonished.

I was born, a girl, several months later. I am now
teaching the history of religions at a university.

(Miss Ryu)

A girl's *yin* dives down.

COLORFUL FISH

My boarding-house keeper said, "A beautiful fish appeared from a river. Taking a parasol with it, it glided up through a field of flowers."

After the dream her daughter was born. She joked, "My beautiful daughter replaced the fish."

(Mr. Chŏng, student)

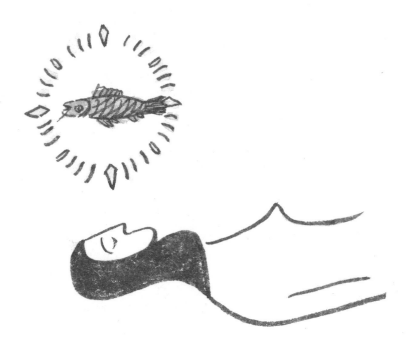

A fish has flexibility. Your baby will glide safely through the tides of life.

CARP

My family took a journey to Sŏrak Mountain, which was dark green and heavily wooded in summer. While we were climbing up, many kinds of birds were flying and singing in front of us.

We arrived at a waterfall, perhaps Piryong Falls. Clear waters were falling from above. I was paddling a small boat through the water. All of a sudden, a school of carp came down the falls. They were big and very lively. My heart leapt. I stopped paddling in order to catch them. After doing so, I was pleased, and woke up.

I bore a son. Very healthy, handsome and bright at nine months old, he likes looking at books and listening to music.

(Mrs. Kang, teacher)

A boy is "big," and "lively."
Carp dreams: 69% 男. A carp, especially a gold or red one, is considered a model of virility.

CATFISH

My mother knelt by a cold spring, filling up a pot with water. Then she saw a catfish.

She caught it, and put it in the pot. But the spring became very dry. Mother was very surprised. So she put the catfish back in the spring, and the water came back again.

She gave birth to a boy, me. A cold spring is very clean. The catfish is the master of the fish in the spring, so I may become a master in society.

(Mr. Chŏng, student)

A wavy moustache grows from a boy.
By putting the fish back, his mother was blessed.

DOLPHIN

One night, my sister-in-law was strolling to the sea. It looked very deep and blue. The sky did, too. A pine forest was by the sea. White sand covered the beach. It was wide and clean. My sister-in-law ran barefoot across the sands like a child.

Shortly after, she was fishing in the sea for a little dolphin. It was so pretty and cute. Its nose and mouth glittered. They glared in the sun, so she could barely open her eyes and look at them.

After a while, she was on a large playground by herself. She ran without stopping along the margin of the grounds. And the dolphin chased after her, hopping like a rabbit. She raced away and it followed her for a long time. At last, she fell to the ground, hugging the dolphin tightly with a smile.

She had a son.

(Anon., teacher)

Chasing and "hopping" come from a boy's energy.
In another dream, a dolphin boy rescued a woman from pirates at sea.

GOLDFISH

My aunt was strolling along the coast early in the morning. Suddenly a carp arose, swimming towards her through the sea. Surprised, she fled away.

But a crowd of people around her told her that it was a rare carp, and to "Grasp it." So she strode back, and

94

embraced it in her arms.

She brought it home and put it in a fish bowl. Surprisingly, it changed into a goldfish!

Ten months later, she gave birth to a girl. Her daughter was cute and smart in her childhood. She is now a doctor in the U.S.A., and a mother.

(Miss Pang, student)

A girl is kept safely inside, because the world is full of dangers, and watched over by her parents.

Goldfish dreams: 60% 女.

OCTOPUS

I was hurrying by the seaside in a white, Korean dress. It was windy and rainy. I was trying to escape from a very big octopus and a turtle, but they caught up with me and I fell into the sea.

Finally I gave up. I was crying, and woke up.

After seven months, my daughter was born. She is one year old, and vivacious.

(Anon, teacher)

Yin wind and rain accompany a passionate girl.

SHELLFISH

One day, my father set out to sea rowing a boat. In the moonlight, the calm sea was golden. He stretched out a net to catch fish, and later, he towed it out of the water. But, instead of fish, he found a lot of pearl oysters.

He took the oysters home.

Of course a pearl oyster means a girl, but his dream of me seems extraordinary, because a lot of oysters mean fame.

When I was a child, I was very pretty like a doll. My father believed I would be Miss Korea. But little by little, growing up, I changed into an unattractive, short and fat girl. My father's hope is slowly disappearing. But I want to say that I am young and my life is not at an end yet.
(Miss Chang, student)

An oyster's shell is associated with the secrets of a vagina. Shellfish dreams: 70% 女.

SNAIL

My mother told me, "It was early spring. There was still some unmelted snow, and I was walking along the bank around a rice field in the evening. In the field there was limpid water due to the thaw.

Just below the calm surface of the water were many fresh-water snails. So I bent low and began gathering them up in my skirt.

I came back home with a skirt filled with snails."
I was born. I am a quick-tempered girl, but optimistic.
(Miss Yang, student)

The charms of a girl are concealed, as in a shell.
A snail's horns give her quick-temper. Its spiral shape, optimism.

WHALE

A great white whale was playing with my mother in the sea. After a while it shrank, getting smaller and smaller until it swam into her ear.

I, her son, have a mild personality.
(Anon., boy student)

"Great" means a boy: "white," long life.

96

"Smaller...ear," is the way to the womb.

AMPHIBIANS AND REPTILES

CROCODILE

One fine summer day, my wife dreamed she was caught (swimming) in a downpour. The rain was falling on the sea, which was filled with shoals of fish. Three women were talking. "Who is the swimmer with the pretty dress?," asked one.

Suddenly the seashore was crowded with people. Many advised my wife, "Don't dive in the sea. Come here out of the water."

Just then some of the fishes changed into crocodiles. All the people prayed. It was a solemn sight.

We had a son. A generous child, he plays with a girl cousin.

(Mr. Pae, teacher)

The sea is "generous." A crocodile is analogous to a dragon, which is usually a boy in birth dreams.

DRAGON

"The Chinese Dragon is a strange mixture of several animals. Ancient native writers...inform us that it has the head of a camel, the horns of a stag, the eyes of a demon, the ears of a cow, the neck of a snake, the belly of a clam, the scales of a carp, the claws of an eagle, and the soles of a tiger. On its head is the *chi'ih nuh* lump that (like a 'gas-bag') enables it to soar through the air."

(Donald Mackenzie, *Myths of China and Japan*)

Also, according to Mackenzie, a watersnake transforms into a scaly dragon after 1,500 years, grows a horn after another 500 years, and after 1,000 more years sprouts wings.

A dragon is rarely seen by human beings because it changes colors, chameleon-like, from black (water) to blue (sky or trees) to yellow (earth) to red (sun) to white (air) to gold (Heaven), etc., according to its surroundings.

Dragons were a sign of Imperial authority in China and Korea, and kings sat upon the "Dragon Throne." To score high on a civil service examination was to "pass through the Dragon's Gate" and get a position in the government.

Dreams of dragons are the most common birth dreams for boys, and about 84% of all dragon dreams concern them.

To dream of a dragon could mean the blessings of Heaven upon an unborn child, and such a dream could legitimate the founder of a kingdom as it did Kao-tsu, who organized an army which helped him establish the Han dynasty of China in 206 B.C. Prior to his birth his mother dreamt that a dragon appeared before her, and she made love with it next to a large pond.
(Mrs. Wang Su-yi, professor)

Birth dreams of a dragon coming out of a pond and consorting with a young woman are being dreamed by Koreans even today. For instance:

My mother was climbing a mountain one day, and she saw a rainbow in a valley. After a few minutes, she found a pond of boiling water, and began to wash her hair.

While doing so, she saw a giant dragon. She wandered off with it, surprised at herself.

It rained, causing her to awake.

My sister was born. She is clear-minded, tall and like an angel. She studied art at the university, and seems happy.

(Miss Kwon, student)

The word for "dragon" in Korean is *yong* which is also colloquial for "penis;" so dragons generally herald boys; yet here, a girl was born because of the "rainbow in the valley," which describes the nourishing potential of the female organ. She, however, has the masculine quality of being "tall."

It might be assumed that many early legends of the births of famous Koreans, mostly found in the *Samguk Yusa,*—like Aryong, first queen of Shilla, from under "the left (female) side of a dragon's ribs,"—were also derived from birth dreams.

Yi I (Yulgok) (1536-1584) was an eminent Neo-Confucian philosopher and social reformer. He sought moral principles through experience in the outside world as well as by wide study. Koreans recall him today as "a man of pure heart and clean hands."

One day, in a dream, his mother ventured into a big, dark cave by herself. All at once she was afraid and tried her best to escape from the cave, but couldn't. Her skin was drenched with sweat. And because she was already pregnant, she was hugging her abdomen and praying, "Please help me!" Soon she felt at ease and her body was glistening. She escaped, only to find herself in front of a very wide sea. As she was standing there, suddenly quite a large dragon appeared, and she watched it rising toward the sky. Unexpectedly the dragon turned, swooping down into her breast.

A month later, her child was born.

(Mrs. So, teacher)

The anonymously authored *Un-gae Pillow* varies the above story, saying that a black dragon was living under the deep sea. Then he jumped to the surface and into her bedroom.

Interestingly enough, according to the same source, after Yi's death, the family saw a black dragon jump to the heavens through the ceiling.

Rhee Syng-man was a leader in the anti-Japanese Occupation movement, and the first "democratically" elected President of Korea (July 20, 1948).

This is a rendering of his mother's birth dream :

She was already forty years old, but had borne only daughters. A Methodist, she was praying every day to her "Father in Heaven" for a son, but couldn't have one.

One night, she dreamt she was walking in the forest, with no special purpose, when suddenly a dragon flew down from the heavens, rushing into her heart.

Very surprised, she woke up.

On March 26, 1875, the baby was born.

She named him "Meet the Dragon," because of her dream. Later, when he was ten, due to his difficulties in early life, she changed his name to "Late Flowering."

(Mr. Kim Young-jo, professor)

What follows may be the most fabulous bevy of dragon dreams ever assembled.

I

One day, my friend's mother was washing clothes by a well. Suddenly a great blue dragon came down from above with a thunderous, flash of lightning. It belched fire from his mouth into the well. My friend's mother was very surprised and fainted away.

A short time later, when she awoke (still dreaming) there was a bright light in the well. She looked down and saw a big, white egg inside. She pulled it up and embraced it, but it broke.

My friend was born. His name is "Myŏng-yong," meaning "Bright Dragon." He is now an officer in the Air Force. He plans to be a pilot and fly up high in the sky like a dragon.

(Mr. Hwang, student)

The "well" is his mother's womb.
A "bright light" and "big" indicate a boy.

2

A massive golden dragon was flying over to me when a noisy electronic wave almost broke my eardrums. I fled in horror. Then the dragon landed in the chicken coop beside me, laying several eggs on the ground, and sitting there inside the fence with its long body around them and its big head up.

The eggs looked like dark brown beans with strong shells of unimaginable size. I tried breaking them with my teeth, but they were too strong.

My wife had already been pregnant for three or four months. We had a boy. He is optimistic and active in everything, and is doing very well in middle school.

(Mr. Kim, teacher)

"Strong" and "unimaginable size" describe a boy.

3

My friend's mother dreamed that she and her husband were sitting in a room. While talking to each other, my

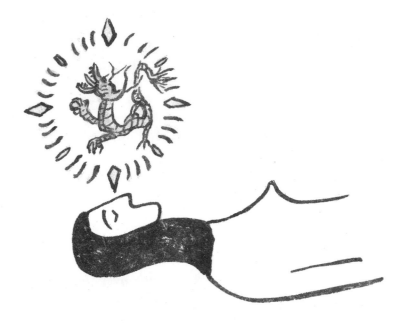

A dragon has magical powers. Your baby will fill up the gap between Heaven and earth with its talents.

friend's mother sensed something was outside. Upon opening the door to see what it was, she was surprised to find a huge bag.

Perplexed, she brought it into the room, and opened it carefully, taking out a ball-like object.

"What is it?" She asked her husband.

"It is a dragon's horn."

It was soft and smooth. They put it into the bag and she carried it in her arms. She put it on the shelf and they looked at the bag all the time.

After this, she woke up.

My friend is a kind and sympathetic girl.

(Miss Sǒ, student)

A girl is preciously "ball-like," inside a container, and put safely on a "shelf" for her parents to wonder at.

A dragon has no ears, so its horns are for hearing.

4

One day, my mother walked to the high school in her neighborhood. That school had a lot of green grass in the playground. My mother laid down comfortably on the grass. The sky was very blue.

Two dragons came up to her. Each gave her a lit lamp, and they said, "We will fight each other. The winner will receive a lit lamp from you as a prize."

My mother was very frightened at their sight. Shivering, she was unwilling to hold the lit lamps in her hands.

The dragons fought violently with each other. My mother closed her eyes out of fear.

When she opened her eyes, one of the dragons came up to her and said, "I am a female dragon. I am the winner." And holding a lit lamp on her long tongue, she slowly disappeared.

Curiously, the other lit lamp, in my mother's left hand, lost its light by itself. Breathless with fear, she suddenly woke up.

A girl was born, me.

(Miss Lee, teacher)

5

My mother saw a serpent hanging from the branch of a tree. He beseeched her to cut his head off. My mother was trembling like a leaf. But the serpent persisted, saying, "Please cut off my head, so I can become a dragon and be able to fly up in the sky."

When my mother heard this, she cut his neck with a

knife. The moment she did so, the snake became a dragon and flew up in the sky. Then she awoke.

My brother was born. When he was four years old, he fell into boiling water and badly burned his leg. The scar still remains. He's in college now, has a clear head and is very talented.

(Mrs. Lee, teacher)

A boy's power flies "up in the sky."

6

In the middle of the night, my mother was wandering deep in a forest. In the darkness, she saw a brilliant light on the ridge of a distant mountain and strode in haste towards the flickering spot. As she was approaching, it was getting brighter. At last it became bright like day. Before her was a glittering crystal, called a *Yŏŭiju*.

My mother wrapped it up in her long skirt, but while walking down the harsh mountain road she came across an enormous serpent. Although my mother wanted to possess the crystal, she became familiar with the snake's pressing situation, that is, a snake is supposed to become a dragon and fly up to the sky after praying for one thousand years. So she gave him the glowing stone.

All at once the snake changed into a glistening, golden dragon in the mysterious and beautiful fog and flew up into the sky with my mother on his head.

I, a son, was born. As the snake turns into a dragon after a long period of prayer in the dense forest, I can also be a person of worth by studying steadily day by day.

(Mr. Yun, student)

A dream shows potential, but the child still must strive to realize it.

7

I found a lake in the forest. It was boiling. I gazed at it from behind a tree, surprised at the sight. A dragon was ascending to Heaven. I could contain my surprise no more and blurted out, "A dragon is going to Heaven!"

Meanwhile, the dragon fell down into the lake. Then an old Taoist hit me on the head. He scolded me, saying, "A woman shouldn't mutter when a dragon is going to Heaven." I ran away so surprised, not believing what I had seen.

The next day, I dreamed a dragon was going to Heaven with a glass bead in his mouth.

I couldn't contain my amazement, muttering again. But the moment I muttered, the dragon fell down into the lake!

My child was a boy.

My son was very clever and intelligent. He studied on his own, graduated from Seoul National University and worked at a research institute.

After that, he married and lived happily, But one day, climbing Halla Mountain, he fell from a cliff and was crippled.

Now separated from his wife, he lives alone with a housekeeper.

(Mrs. Ko, housewife)

A dragon wishes to realize his potential, carrying his "glass bead" of power to Heaven, but there are dangers on the way. Nobody should see him ascending.

8

My mother was walking around a lake in her dream. A big rock was by the lake. Suddenly an old man wearing white clothes appeared out of the water, and said, "Don't be afraid of me. You will have a grandson. I will give you his name." As soon as he said this, he turned into a dragon, flew up into the sky and quickly disappeared. The name "Kuk-hŏn" was written on the rock. *Kuk* means "Nation." *Hŏn* means "Constitution." My son, "Kuk-hŏn", is ten years old now. He is very smart, and I believe he will be a great statesman.

(Mrs. Na, teacher)

9

A strange woman in white clothes was crossing through the heavy rain, coming to my mother's home. She did not have an umbrella. She called my mother by name, and with a gesture of her hand, said, "Follow me!" Soon she disappeared into a pond.

At the same time, the rain stopped. My mother saw a resplendent rainbow shining brightly around the water.

After a while she plunged into the pond, swimming to the bottom where she met the Dragon King. After bowing to him, she sat on his knees. The Dragon King gave her a package, saying, "This will be your offspring."

Thanking him, my mother swam back up, and awoke. It was my mother's dream of me.

(Miss Ch'a, student)

A "resplendent rainbow" graces a colorful daughter of the Dragon King.

The king lives in a gorgeous underwater palace and feeds on pearls.

10

It is autumn, a fine day, but raining lightly. A gentle breeze is blowing. A beautiful woman (the dreamer) is

sleeping with her husband in a Buddhist temple.
After a while, she gets up and opens the door. She looks
out at the mountain valley. The prospect from the top of
the mountain is very beautiful and delicate. She takes a
deep breath of fresh air.

Down below the mountain, something is moving, like a
black blot. It gets bigger and bigger, and changes into a
small snake. Then the snake changes into a huge dragon.
The dragon becomes two dragons: one blue, and the
other yellow. They put small balls in their mouths, which
are glittering.

While she is amazed and frightened, her husband gets
up, and looks out the door to see them rising in the sky.
Suddenly the blue one flies closer.

Surprised, they close the door hastily, but the dragon
breaks into the room, coiling around her husband's body.
Astonished, she tries to uncoil it and open its mouth.

After a good while, the dragon slips out of the room
and rises into the sky.

A son was born ten months later. He has a colorful
personality, and is a teacher.

(Anon., teacher)

A son may wrestle with his father, for two *yangs* compete with
each other.

II

One day, my mother was sitting in her family grave-
yard, wearing a white, mourning dress. Her grandmother's
and grandfather's tombs were there. The hill descended
slowly towards the sea. No sound could be heard and
nothing could be seen. She felt like escaping, because she
was seized with fear.

Standing up, she saw something like smoke, but it

107

wasn't smoke. It was a dragon! Wriggling, it approached her. At last it plunged through her mourning dress. She fell unconscious.

My older brother was born. He is over-sensitive and has everything his own way. He is now running a private school.

(Anon., teacher)

A son may plunge passionately through his mother's dress, because *yin* and *yang* attract one another.

12

My elder sister was climbing a mountain with her friends. Suddenly shrouded by fog, her friends disappeared. She shouted for them, but nobody responded. She was afraid and tried to descend in a hurry, but could not find the way down.

She was so afraid that she collapsed on the spot, starting to cry loudly.

After crying for a long time she felt thirsty. But there wasn't a fountain anywhere. She wandered around for a while. Finally, she discovered a giant fountain in the fog.

The discovery of water delighted her. She drank in a hurry.

Suddenly, as the fountain split in two, a giant dragon rose up out of it, but soon disappeared.

She awoke with surprise.

A boy was born the next day. He's still a baby.
(Miss Yu, student)

A male rises like a "giant" geyser generated by heat.

13

One cold winter's day, when the sun was shining with

chilly brightness, my mother was standing before a mountain. To her wonderment, the peak appeared to be covered with something. It was a dragon!

All at once it began moving. It lay itself down on the mountain. Its belly was facing up to the sky, and it suddenly radiated with gold light. My mother awoke.

I was born a boy. A villager said, "The baby will become the best of men."

(Mr. Lim, student)

14

Going somewhere, my landlady was suddenly surrounded by a heavy fog. In a few minutes, the fog disappeared and before her eyes a stairway with uncountable steps wound upwards.

She rose up the stairs easily, and at the top she saw a very large tree which almost touched the sky. A monstrous yellow dragon that was holding a red gem in its mouth wound about the tree.

Then it flew up into the sky. Afraid, she woke up.

After a few days, she conceived, and later bore a son. He is good-hearted, a middle school student.

(Mr. Han, student)

15

Around my house, white clouds rose up one after another. A blue dragon was flying among them. My father wanted to grasp the dragon's breasts, so he jumped up and caught hold of them. As soon as he did so he came out of his dream.

The child was my younger sister, who is in middle school.

She is healthy and has a good appetite. She has a

boyish personality.
(Anon., student)

A female dragon, naturally, has breasts.

16

My father and his landlord were harvesting rice in a field when suddenly they spotted a big dragon flying to the sky. Though they were extremely surprised, the landlord threw his sickle up at the dragon and struck its belly. White blood spilled out, pouring all over my father, and he woke up.

My mother gave birth to a boy in her own house. The landlady was helping her, and cut the umbilical cord with a sickle. According to Korean tradition, this is supposed to bless the child with a long life. But my younger brother died the next day. I think the sickle was rusty and gave him tetanus.

(Mr. Kim, student)

A dream can warn of a real life danger, but it must be heeded to do any good.

17

My mother was playing with her friends in a field near a stream. Suddenly they saw several dragons descending from the sky. The women were all frightened and suspicious, though mystified.

They ran to the place where the dragons were landing. My mother's friends raced ahead of her, but she caught up.

Presently my mother reached the spot, and unfolded her skirt in order to catch the dragons. Fortunately, she managed to catch one of them, red and very thin.

Ten months later she produced a son. He is tall and handsome, but thin.

(Anon., teacher)

After realizing their power in Heaven, dragons return to earth to offer their graces.

18

My mother caught a flying dragon, and sealed it in a big jar.

After a while, she heard a queer sound, and going outdoors found an animal whose upper body was that of a woman and whose lower body was a dragon's.

She woke up in surprise.

Ten months later, a girl was born. She is soft, calm and a teacher.

(Miss Kim, teacher)

SNAKE

Today, in efforts to bolster their legitimacy, political leaders in Asia still point to birth dreams, as did newly elected, Korean President Roh Tae-woo:

As his mother hadn't had a son after seven years of marriage, she and her mother-in-law prayed for one at Hwa-gae Temple up on a mountain near Taegu.

At dawn, on the last day of their three day vigil, a big blue snake wrapped around his mother's body in a dream.

(*Joong-ang Daily News,* Election Day, December 16, 1987)

About the same time, Roh's grandmother dreamt that she visited a temple and received a black bead from an old monk.

(Sŏk Sŏng-u, *T'aegyo*)

Blue is the color of the East, where Korea is in relation to China, "The Middle Kingdom." A large blue snake, which is possibly a dragon, symbolizes Korean royalty. A president is the modern equivalent of a king.

A monk Tongmyŏng said, "The bead is a *Yŏŭiju*, a 'wishfulfilling gem' which grows in a dragon's throat, and gives the one who possesses it power to do whatever he pleases."

Public knowledge of such dreams inspires others to hope for, and to have auspicious birth dreams of their own.

I

My mother had been married for eight years, but wasn't able to bear any children. Her parents-in-law scolded her every day because she hadn't given birth to a son. She prayed at many shrines, and in particular, before one penis-shaped stone, dedicated to the Seven Stars (Big Dipper) god.

Every morning before dawn, she would get up, and wash her hair and body in clear water. She would leave the house, without having eaten anything, about 5 a.m., and walk through the countryside for about two hours to the stone, where she would pray, for it was believed that the god came down into that stone and gave the spirit of a son to a faithful woman. She would continue praying all day long and returned home about 10 p.m. She kept on doing this for "100 days (i.e., an auspicious period)," even in the cold winter, until finally, while at home, she had a dream:

She was coming home from her daily routine of prayer when a big, yellow snake crossed the road in front of her. She woke up, and soon found that she had indeed conceived. I was that child, her son.

My mother continued going to the stone, once a year on my birthday, giving offerings of rice and wine to the god. Now she has passed away, but I still visit that stone sometimes, and give my thanks to the Seven Stars.

(Mr. Chŏng, businessman)

A "big" snake is a boy. My own wife dreamed a small wriggly snake crawled across the bedroom floor and bit her on the arm. She bore our daughter.

Dreams of snakes are by far the most frequent birth dreams : 59% 男.

2

Mother said,

"I was watching
a crab
in a pond. . . .

It changed
into a flower
snake

and crept
up to me.

"Soon our beautiful
daughter was born."

(Mrs. Kang, teacher)

A "flower" snake is banded red, yellow and black, and almost always is a colorful girl.

3

Our forefathers lived in hamlets at the feet of mountains. Their livelihood depended on the earth. They had to cultivate it, so they needed a strong man to farm it.

When a woman married a farmer, the mother-in-law expected her to bear a strong son. My grandmother was thus concerned about bearing a son. She and her husband worked hard in the field until late, and dusk came. After dinner she went to bed fatigued. Strangely her body was almost exhausted, but her mind was clear while dreaming:

She was wandering in the deep, misty woods. By a stream, she felt thirsty. When she knelt down and was about to bend forward to gulp a mouthful of water, she saw the reflection of a large snake in the water.

She was so surprised that she screamed out, swirling her hand desperately. She got up, soaking her body

A snake is intelligent and sensual. Your baby will exercise his brain and body for success in life.

114

thoroughly.

Looking around, she realized it was a birth dream. How happy she was! But she couldn't tell anybody, not even her husband, because of tradition.

She had a son. He was clever, and strong.

(Mr. Pak, student)

Thirst is caused by *yang* "fire." A boy is "large."
A snake is "clever."

4

One muggy, summer evening my mother was taking a bath in a stream by some trees. As it was getting dark, she finished bathing soon and started for home. On her way through the forest, she met a strange old man who was dressed in white. He begged her to give him something to eat, but she had nothing. As he drew nearer, she was surprised by how ugly and monstrous his face was. Horrified, she couldn't even take one step back.

While she was turning away, the old creature was transformed into a big, long snake. It was white with black stripes. Strange to say, it was friendly. While she hesitated, it crawled over to her and up her body to her neck. It dipped its head down the back of her clothes, and crept inside, twining around her, but its body felt sweet and comfortable.

She gave birth to my sister three months later. According to her, "A white and black snake symbolizes a female, and a yellow one a male."

(Mrs. Hwang, teacher)

A girl hugs affectionately.

5

The sky was blue, without a speck of cloud, and the sun was shining brightly. A breeze was stirring the trees and flowers. As it was ideal spring weather, my mother went for a walk. Here and there, girls by twos and threes were gathering herbs. They were beautiful girls, and wearing brilliant, white clothes like angels.

My mother passed them, walking on and on.

After continuing a long time, she found herself standing where she had never been before. There she saw a couple of snakes crawling through the grass. One was female and the other male. My mother gobbled up the male. Pretty soon she woke up, finding herself in bed.

The following day, she gave birth to a little girl. The daughter is kind, gentle and bright.

(Miss Yŏ, student)

The mother was in a feminine atmosphere of "beautiful girls" and "flowers." Her desire for a son was already thwarted by destiny.

TOAD

One day, my mother bent down by the stream to wash clothes. While washing, she suddenly found a big toad seated on the rocks. The toad was very big and different from normal ones. Thinking this strange, she stopped her work and edged up very close to it.

Generally a toad is afraid of people who come up close to it, but this one sat calmly on the rock without fear. My mother, as if by magic, wrapped the toad up in her long skirt.

After the dream, she got pregnant. Depending on a

legendary birth dream, she thought the baby would surely be a son. So, when I was born, my parents were very deeply disappointed at my being a girl.

But now they love me very much and I love them with all my heart.

(Miss Kim, student)

A girl sits quietly, with hidden "magic," by the wash.

The legend may have been that of Kŭmwa, a handsome boy who resembled a golden frog in the *Samguk Yusa*. He was discovered under a big stone by a king, who adopted him as his heir.

Regardless of the Korean belief that "a toad has the face of a handsome boy," 60% of the dreams of toads are 女. This is because toads are sluggish, or *yin*, and give off a mess of water when you pick them up.

Frogs, on the other hand, being lively, turn out to be boys.

2

A woman, I read about in a book, dreamed there was a persimmon tree in her back yard. Under the tree a golden toad was sluggishly playing. It had three horns on its head. Inspecting it, she kicked it unintentionally. Worried that she might have hurt it, she immediately picked it up and carried it into her room. She, then, closed the door and went out. After a while, when she returned and opened the door, she couldn't find the toad. "Maybe it escaped," she thought.

After ten months she gave birth to a handsome son. She raised him very carefully. But when he was two years old, he got sick and died.

In this dream, the toad's three horns meant he would have three talents. But as his mother kicked him, he got sick. When she opened the door and couldn't see him, it meant that he might die early.

(Mrs. Pak, teacher)

Special qualities of this toad make him a boy: "golden" is the color of Heaven. A horn is a phallic symbol; "three" is an odd, *yang* number. It also displays the graces of Heaven, earth and man, like a crown.

TURTLE

A sea-turtle is viewed as the noble minister of the Dragon King, especially if he has three tails. In one folk tale-like birth dream, a woman teacher said, "I was strolling along the sea, one fine day, and saw three boys ahead of me arguing about something between their feet. Drawing nearer, I saw that it was a turtle with three tails and it had a gold crown on its head. The boys were arguing as to who would cut off its head and take it home to eat. I begged the boys to leave it alone and they finally agreed to do so.

After this, the turtle said to me, "You have saved my life. I am the son of the Dragon King and anything you wish for I will give you. Get on my back and I will ride you along the beach."

But I was afraid to get on his back, lest I fall off. But he reassured me, and though he was small, when I got on, he began to grow bigger and bigger until he was large enough to carry me along.

After this I got pregnant and had a son.
(Mrs. Pae, student)

The Korean word for turtle, *chara,* also is colloquial for "penis," which resembles a turtle's head.

My wife was feeding corn to the chickens in the yard. A small turtle crawled through the yard, crossing by the chickens, while trying to reach my wife. But as it came near, the chickens suddenly attacked it.

When my wife got to the melee, the chickens were already pecking at the turtle's head. Surprised, she quickly picked the turtle up, embraced it, and awoke.

My son was born five months later. But his left ear has a little hole in it, as if the chickens had really pecked it. He is very honest and brave.

(Anon., teacher)

Turtle dreams: 81% 男.

WILD BIRDS

Mrs. Wang Su-yi tells a mythical birth story of Sëeh, the founder of the Shang dynasty (1765-1123 B.C.) in China:

One of emperor K'uh's concubines, whose name was Keen-teih, was trekking across a vast plain and found a black bird's egg all alone on the sand. It was striped with five rainbow-like colors (blue for East, red for South, yellow for Center, white for West, and black for North) and had 800 Chinese characters written on it. She picked it up, put it in a box, covering it with a red cloth. That night, as she lay by its side, she dreamt an angel appeared before her, who said, "If you carry this egg with you, then you will have a very clever son. He will make a very good emperor."

So she carried the egg with her for a year. Then she got pregnant and after fourteen months (an auspicious period of gestation), she gave birth to a boy named Sëeh, who later became a minister in the court of Emperor Yu. For his services, he was granted his own domain, and later became the progenitor of the *Yin* people.

Another version of Sĕeh's story is on the first page of the *Samguk Yusa,* "Legends and History of the Three Kingdoms of Ancient Korea," compiled by the monk, Ilyŏn (born 1206 A.D.), along with other tales of the miraculous births of famous Chinese emperors. It says that Sĕeh's mother dreamt that she swallowed an egg dropped by a black bird. Another Chinese version, related by my colleague, Professor Chang Shao-wen, describes her first praying for a son, then taking a bath in a river and swallowing a vari-colored egg dropped by a swallow. Swallowing is a magical way to draw a baby into the womb and occurs frequently in birth dreams.

Ancient myths often influence modern dreams:

A big black bird was flying high in the blue sky, carrying a spherical egg in its beak. Suddenly it cried out loudly and the egg dropped to the ground.
Ten days later, I was born.
(Mr. Ha, student)

MYTHICAL BIRDS

I

*A bear-
eagle*

*perched
in a tree*

*suddenly
soars
around,*

*alighting
on my bosom.*

I feel
peace,

for it
is soft,

and light
as down.

A "soft,
light" girl
was born.

(Anon., teacher)

2

I am kneeling in a vast field, and picking many flowers in order to make a pretty necklace. Suddenly I hear a strange sound from the sky, "Hu... Hu... Hu..." Looking up, I see a marvelous animal perched in a huge tree.

It resembles a lion and an eagle with wings, and is very splendid. Its body shoots out bright lights.

Everybody is eager to catch it, but nobody can.

As soon as I open my arms, it flies to me and nestles in my embrace. I feel delighted, as if I have won a victory.

After ten months I bore a lovely daughter.

(Mrs. Yi, housewife)

A "necklace" of "flowers" is a circle of fertility.

CRANE

Before giving birth to Ch'un-hyang, a Korean folk story heroine, her mother dreamt that a beautiful girl, shimmering with the colors of the rainbow and riding a blue crane came flying to her through the air.

(*The Story of a Faithful Wife, Ch'un-hyang*)

In the *Un-gae Pillow*, an anonymous collection of birth dreams, compiled during the Japanese Occupation of Korea (1910-1945), we find a colorful dream for Eun Jung-hwa, an official in the court of King Hyojong (1649-1659). His father dreamed an old man was standing before him. He wore the wings of a crane, and had feathers on his head like those of a copper pheasant. In his hand was a light stick and his shoes were made of clouds. This man told him, "Your baby will be born by an order of the king."

After saying this, the old man disappeared, leaving the father very surprised.

At the time of birth, the shadow of a cloud appeared on the door, though the sky was clear, and a sweet fragrance pervaded the room.

A crane was flying down from the sky. As soon as she saw it, my neighbor spread out her skirt and welcomed it. After a while, it turned into a cock.

When her grandfather saw this, he directed her to carry it to the kettle and boil it. So she put it in and lit a fire. Then the cock turned into a human being.

Surprised, she plucked it out of the kettle. But its hip had been burnt off. She did not know what to do. Then it changed back into a crane, and flew up into the sky.

A crane has a firm purpose. But a crane turning into a cock means a change of personality. My neighbor's daughter was heroic. But in her thirties she developed a violent temper because of her husband's mistreatment.

However, she happened to meet a preacher. After that, she was absorbed in a life of faith. She had a right-minded nature again. But she also had a chronic disease,

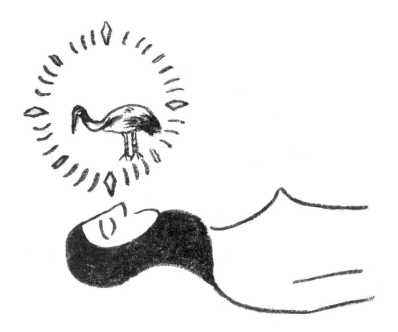

A crane has a long, wise life. Your child will be a dreamy sage.

nephritis, which grew worse, and she died early.

The grandfather in the dream symbolizes the preacher. The burnt hip represents the nephritis, growing worse. And the human changing into a crane and flying off reflects her death.

(Miss Sŏ, student)

A girl flies into the "kitchen," a place traditionally taboo for boys.

Crane dreams: 79% 男, because cranes have long, *yang* bodies.

DOVE

While a clear sun rose in the very blue sky, throwing light on all places, my mother got up and was cooking breakfast. Fire was roaring in the big fireplace and from the large iron kettle white smoke rose up in thick clouds.

Just then, a white dove flapped into the kitchen and sat on her lap. She looked at the dove, patting her on the head and said, "You are such a beautiful dove. Are you starving? Will you have some rice?"

The dove nodded her head, assenting. My mother stood up, stepped over to the large caldron, and opened its lid. The rice was properly done, so she threw some to the dove. The dove ate, and then sailed away to the east, where the sun rises.

My mother conceived my elder sister. A dove, as you know, is a symbol of peace. Rice and fire are symbolic of riches and honors. Because it throws light on the world, the sun is a symbol of service to others. Well, my sister is very beautiful and graceful like the dove in my mother's dream. She grew up without fighting with her friends or making any trouble.

(Miss Chang, student)

A girl sits in "the kitchen" by mother, nodding docilely.

A white dove is almost always a sign of a pure-hearted, filial girl, but a common pigeon is usually a boy.

EAGLE

A couple had lived a life of good deeds, but they were growing old and had not been able to produce a son. They journeyed to a mountain temple and prayed for one.

After this the wife dreamt of a bird, bigger than an eagle, flying in the sky. It suddenly flew down into their house. Soon she became pregnant and had a son in 1127 A.D.

The boy was named Yueh-fei, "Big Bird," after the one in the dream. Such a fabulous bird can fly 10,000 miles and not get tired, and so is a leader of birds.

Thus, Yueh-fei grew up to be a heroic general serving the Sung dynasty in China.

(Mr. Chang Shao-wen, professor)

I

While I was looking for a building on the street I noticed all the passers-by were looking up in the sky and I looked up, too. What a surprise! A large golden bird, which resembled an eagle, but bigger and a little different —was roving over our heads. People were surprised and expressed admiration and respect for it, and someone called it, "the Grandfather of all birds." I was overwhelmed by the beautiful sight.

Suddenly the bird, which had been soaring so admirably, came down exhausted, folding its wings on the top of a building, which I then tried to enter. I ran up to the top while the spectators shouted. I, then, saw the bird's sorrowful eyes. I had never seen, or felt such deep pangs of despair before.

While I was standing there, a young nurse, wearing a white gown, approached me and shouted, "It's because of you." I was surprised and woke up.

I told the dream to my husband. We decided to cancel a scheduled abortion, and to keep the child I wasn't sure I could take care of. We had a lovely son. He is two years old now. He had teeth early, walked early and spoke early. He doesn't forget anything he learns.

(Mrs. Shim, teacher)

A boy is inspiringly, "large golden," and seen "on top."

2

My mother was wandering along a road through a thick forest. No one was about. The sky was fair, without wind. Suddenly, as if from nowhere, a host of birds covered the sky. Among them, my mother could see an eagle, a skylark, a sparrow, a wild goose, a magpie, a pheasant and other kinds she didn't know.

While she was continuing on, the birds rose above her, circling around in the sky. As she reached her house, the eagle swooped out of the flock, into her bosom, and she woke up.

I was conceived after this dream. When a member of my family talks about the birth dream, they say, "You will be a prodigy."

(Mr. Kim, student)

An eagle is the most manly of birds.

HAWK

My elder sister was traveling on an unknown country road by many trees to meet her husband, whose ancestors' ceremony was going to be held in his hometown. Suddenly, many people rushed into town to escape the attack of a large hawk, which was flying swiftly in the sky. Everyone was frightened, but my sister was less so than the others, because she had a magic pole which could reach up to the sky. She bravely swished it with all her might.

Although the pole was short, it could extend out as far

as she wished it to go. Finally, snaring the hawk, she shouted with horror, "Help me, I've got it, but it's too heavy for me to carry by myself. Help me, darling!" She shouted and shouted, but nobody heard her.

Her husband woke her, "What's happening to you?"

"I had a birth dream. I'm sure the baby will be a boy!"

It was a boy. Although modest, he has sharp eyes. He will enter high school soon.

(Anon., teacher)

A boy's wings fly "high" and "swiftly."

ORIOLE

While I was facing a vast blue void, a yellow oriole, such as the ones which fluttered in the treetops around our house in the spring, was falling through the air before me. It peered in my eyes as if to say, "I'm sorry, but I can't help it," and vanished below. I suddenly felt lonely.

A few days later, my wife, who was three months pregnant, suffered a miscarriage.

(F.J. Seligson)

This dream of our baby's death persuaded me that the baby "spirit" in a dream is a separate entity from the dreamer.

PHOENIX

Shun was a faithful and sagacious advisor to emperor Yao for twenty eight years, and after was chosen to succeed him as emperor of China. He ruled from 2255 to 2206 B.C. Before he was born, his father dreamt that a phoenix appeared before him, holding a grain of rice in its beak. It told him, "My name is Chicken. I will become your son."

He woke up thinking, "That was a very strange dream."

(Mr. Chang Shao-wen, professor)

A phoenix comes from the South and is the bird of rebirth, born out of its own ashes. A phoenix-child, like Shun, will also be reborn out of the fire of his own success.

The following Korean dream has a chicken-phoenix similarity.

My wife said, "I walked to my neighbor's chicken coop to steal a cock. There I saw a big, beautiful one, so I sneaked in quickly and caught it.

In my hands, it changed into a Chinese phoenix and sang a song with a very beautiful voice."

After this, my wife conceived our child. Very kind and bright, our daughter is a primary school teacher.

(Anon., teacher)

A girl has a "beautiful" voice.

SEAGULL

Sitting on a rock by the seashore, her mother saw many seagulls flying towards her. She thought it very strange. They surrounded her, singing beautifully.

Unawares, she was now sitting on top of a mountain. Her child was a girl, and is now a movie star.

(Miss Oh, student)

Beautiful songs celebrate a girl.

STORK

Kim Pyŏng-yŏn (Kim Satkat) (1807–1856) was a roving Korean poet, distinguished by his wide bamboo hat. His father dreamt that in the eastern sky, a blue star was riding in a stork on his way home. One of the stork's wings was broken in a storm and the star gradually lost its light, falling to the ground with a bang.
(Sŏk Sŏng-u, *T'aegyo*)

This sounds like the biography of wandering poets almost anywhere.

One day I met a big stork, who said to me, "You have to get on me if you want to have a beautiful house in the future." So, following his advice, I straddled his back. We flew to an isolated island where numerous storks were living. I enjoyed myself with them for a long time, singing happily.

After many hours, I learned that my host was the supreme chief of all storks, and then I woke up.

After three months, I was pregnant, and I bore a healthy boy. He is nine years old, in primary school.
(Anon., teacher)

A "big" male bird augurs a boy.

UNNAMED BIRDS

I

My grandmother was relaxing in a garden of many fragrant flowers and trees. While admiring these, she heard some strange sounds, and after searching about found seven baby birds.

She picked them up, one at a time, to put into her clothes, but when she picked up the third, the second flew out.

Afterwards she had seven pretty daughters, but the second died as a baby. They are honest, diligent and kind.

(Anon., teacher)

2

I had been taking a stroll in a large field. Suddenly my surroundings were full of light, and in front of my eyes appeared a brilliant rainbow. There was a beautiful white bird near me. It looked soft and desirable.

I sat closer to the bird and carefully grasped it with my hand. Fortunately it did not escape. I looked closer and felt the tender feathers. I uttered a sigh of admiration, smiled happily and awoke.

After the dream, I became pregnant and bore my daughter. She attends school now. She is bright, kind and composed.

(Mrs. Cho, teacher)

"Rainbow," and "tender" "white" are signs of a talented girl.

WILD BEASTS

BEAR

Myth, recorded in the *Samguk Yusa*, has it that about 4,000 years ago, a she-bear and a tigress were living on a mountain in the far northern part of the Korean peninsula. They were praying to be made human beings. A god, hearing these prayers, came down from Heaven beside a white birch and told them to eat only mugwort and garlic and to retire into a cave for 100 days. They entered the cave, but soon the tigress got bored and gave up her retreat. The she-bear remained, however, and after the requisite time metamorphosed into a human being.

She was lonely though, and prayed for a child. Descending, the god mated with her, and after pregnancy, she gave birth to a gifted boy, whom they named "Tan-gun." He founded the earliest Korean kingdom of Old Chosŏn (about 2333 B.C.), and it is he whom modern Koreans claim as their ancestor. Son of a god and a bear, he was naturally a shaman-king, and probably capable of changing himself back into a bear whenever he wished. So, Koreans are on one side of their family tree descended from bears and on the other, gods.

In what is perhaps the earliest account of a Korean birth dream, the *Samguk Yusa* says that King Suro of Kaya (born from a golden egg in 42 A.D.) and his queen, who had been an Indian (or Thai) princess, had been happily married for several years, and one night each dreamed of a bear. Soon afterwards, the queen found out she was pregnant and she gave birth to a son, Crown Prince Kodŭng (who reigned 199–259).

A bear, being strong and protective of its children, represented an ideal image for a king.

Dreams of bears: 88% 男; an exception was a white bear for a girl.

My grandfather was wandering in the forest. He noticed a fragrance and discovered an orchid. He picked it, smelled it for a while, and then stuck it in his hair.

Trying to catch a butterfly, he chased after it and lost

his way in the deep forest. Suddenly he heard some strange sounds. A tiger appeared, attacking him. It wounded him in several places. He tried to escape. When he looked back, he saw a big bear was behind him.

A cute grandson was born. As he grew older, he became gentle and ambitious. He is a freshman at Seoul National University, majoring in applied fine arts. He wants to design cars and industrial products.

(Mr. Che, student)

An orchid, among flowers, is male. The butterfly, a female desired by the dreamer, since he is a man, escaped. A male tiger attacked and bit the man, because *yangs* don't get along so well. And the bear, being "big," was also male, presaging a son.

"Spirit" symbols can metamorphose several times, maybe at the bidding of the sub-consciously inquiring dreamer, and all together can tell us about various characteristics of a newly arriving child. From this perspective, the "orchid" could suggest a scholar. The "butterfly," gentleness. The "tiger," ambition. And the "bear" stands for the patience it takes for him to succeed in his chosen field of industrial design.

Here the grandfather possibly received the above news of the sex and character of his recently conceived grandchild through "dream telepathy." The grandson's own "spirit" may have sent the message from inside his mother's womb, for the human mind is an energy field which knows no physical limits. It can connect with the field of another, changing trillions of black and white particles into color images, creating microscopic visions or gigantic ones and even plug into the entire universe of which it is already a vital part. Maybe the grandson felt a closer kinship to his grandfather than to his mother, and so reached out to him, or else he chose his grandfather because he was unable to "tune in" to his mother, who may have been, for some reason, ignoring his foetal messages.

BOAR

Ch'oe Ch'i-won (859-910 A.D.), was a noted scholar and

calligrapher in the Korean kingdom of Shilla, who recommended a broader participation of the people in the affairs of the government.

When his mother was still unmarried, a gold, wild pig appeared, and slept with her every night in her dreams. She was surprised and ashamed of this behavior, but at last confessed her dreams to her father. He instructed her to tie a golden thread around the pig's leg the next time it appeared. She did so.

Before dawn, the creature trotted contentedly back to its home. In the morning, her father followed the thread, and located the pig's cave deep in the mountains. He returned to his village and asked a shamaness, "What do pigs hate?" The woman replied, "Pig's blood." So he killed his own pig, and tossed the blood all over the entrance of the gold pig's cave.

After that, his daughter got pregnant and gave birth to the wild pig's baby, Ch'oe Ch'i-won.

(Mr. No, student)

The golden pig may have been an ancestor of a Shilla clan.

This dream reminds one of the golden thread in Greek mythology by which Theseus found his way back out of the Cretan Labyrinth.

I

A wild boar was frolicking on a rugged mountain. He had long tusks and was as big as a bull. All of a sudden, he began galloping towards my mother's house. He charged across the mountain, and over the roofs of many houses, on and on. He ran so fast that he caused the wind to rise.

Hearing the noise, people fled for dear life.

At last, the wild boar dashed into my mother's room,

and she woke up surprised.

According to *Haemongyogyŏl* (a book for interpreting dreams), a wild boar represents wealth. The wild boar's dashing into my mother's house means her fate to bear a son. The loud noise and the boar's size mean the son's rising in the world and gaining fame.

My mother got pregnant with me. The wild boar turned into what I am perhaps due to a destiny arranged in a previous existence. Anyway I love his positive drive, so I live in faith that I can do anything I try to do.

(Mr. Lee, student)

"Long tusks," "as big as a bull" and "loud noises" herald a boy.

2

My mother was surprised to find herself at the bottom of a very deep and dangerous ravine in a dense forest at night. Looking around, she saw a great number of wild boars, and was afraid.

She was confused, and ran away, but many followed her.

She got home to her thatched cottage with difficulty, and many of the boars arrived with her. Before she was aware of it, they went into the front room, and entered the kitchen. They bustled about. Suddenly all of them gave birth to piglets. My mother's house was crowded with wild boars and piglets, until she awoke.

After this, she gave birth to my sister. My mother thinks my sister is a blessed woman.

(Miss Pak, student)

The "very deep ravine" and giving birth to "many piglets" in "the kitchen" reveal a girl's bountiful environment.

DEER

There wasn't even a speck of cloud in the sky. It was mild. A stream was flowing smoothly. Two deer were lapping calmly at the edge.

I spied upon them from behind a giant tree because I thought they might run away if they saw me.

When they quit drinking the water they saw me and ran quickly over to me. I hugged and kissed them.

Seven months later I had a son. He is brave and studious, and just entering primary school.

(Anon., teacher)

Boys can run "quickly."
Mother may conceive a second son later.

ELEPHANT

"...It is said, the Midsummer festival was proclaimed in the City of Kapilavastu, and the people were enjoying the feast. During the seven days before, the full moon the Lady Maha Maya had taken part in the festivity, as free from intoxication as it was brilliant with garlands and perfumes. On the seventh day she rose early and bathed in perfumed water: and she distributed four hundred thousand pieces in giving great largesse. Decked in her richest attire she partook of the purest food: and vowing to observe the Eight Commandments, she entered her beautiful chamber, and lying on her royal couch she fell asleep and dreamt this dream.

The four archangels, the Guardians of the world, lifting her up in her couch, carried her to the Himalaya mountains, and placing her under the Great Sala-tree, seven leagues high, on the Crimson Plain, sixty yojanas broad, they stood respectfully aside. Their queens then came toward her, and taking her to the lake of Anotatta, bathed her to free her from human stains; and dressed her in heavenly garments; and anointed her with perfumes; and decked her with heavenly flowers. Not far from there is the Silver Hill, within which is a golden mansion; in it they spread a heavenly couch, with its head towards the East, and on it they laid her down. Then the future Buddha, who had become a superb white elephant, and was wandering on the Golden Hill, not far from there, descended thence, and ascending the Silver hill, approached her from the North. Holding in his silvery trunk a white lotus flower, and uttering a far-reaching cry, he entered the golden mansion, and thrice doing obeisance to his mother's couch, he gently struck her right side, and seemed to enter her womb.

Thus was he conceived at the end of the Midsummer festival. And the next day, having awakened from her sleep, she related her dream to the raja..."

(*Buddhist Birth Stories,* translated by T.W. Rhys Davids)

Ever since Sakyamuni Buddha came into his mother's dreams personified by a white elephant, mothers of future Buddhist saints have been dreaming of white elephants, too. Another Indian example relates to a Buddhist monk and poet called Varsva:

His father dreamed of a jeweled chair on a white elephant's back. Among the jewels was a bright bead which, as it passed through his door, shined in all directions.

(Sŏk Sŏng-u, *T'aegyo*)

These are dreams of the mother of my own Korean Zen Master, the Venerable Haeam (born as Sunch'ŏn), who died at the age of 99 in 1985: One was of a long bundle of curling white thread, and predicted a long, pure life.

In the other dream, "...a Bodhisattva, riding a white elephant, emerged from the sky's edge and descended to the location of his expectant mother. At that spot was a holy rock adorned with flowers and jewels. Upon this rock the Bodhisattva sat and entered Samadhi. After sitting for some time he arose, reached deeply into his chest and brought out a jar of holy milk. He handed it to the woman-with-child, then disappeared.

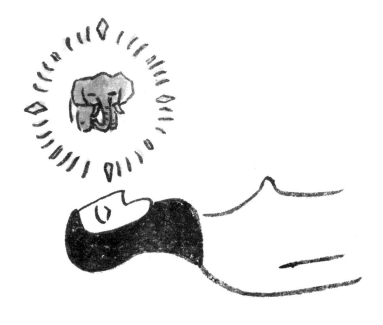

An elephant is strong. Your child will be huge, preforming great physical feasts.

Later that morning, while his mother was giving pain-less birth to Sunch'ŏn, an aura suddenly appeared from nowhere, hovered above the house, and steadfastly abided for some time."

(Recorded by Master Myo-bong in *Gateway to Patriarchal Zen*)

Sakyamuni, starving in his forest meditation, accepted a jar of milk from a worried woman visitor. Perhaps feeling bound by this earthly attachment, he was now giving it back, in the form of a holy son, Haeam, not to her only, but to the world.

Strangely, after Haeam's death, during his cremation at Sudŏk Temple, I glanced up and saw a rainbow aura just overhead, around the sun. Where did he go?

1

My husband was stroking a big white elephant all over its body, and trunk.

A girl was born. She is now a pop music star.

(Lady at Korea Woman's Institute)

Universally, a man feels physically close to a daughter. "White" skin, here, is female beauty.

Maybe the trunk became a microphone.

2

I was wandering on a small mountain. A swift current was running down the slopes and I raced freely alongside it.

When I had descended, a friend called to me. As the stream was between us, I couldn't go to him. So I walked the other way.

A half-destroyed village was beside the path. I sat on the ground to rest. Suddenly some very big elephants appeared, rushing furiously at me, but, somehow, I felt safe. For some time I was in danger, but I was unafraid, and awoke.

My wife gave birth to a boy. He is still a baby. (Anon., teacher)

Boys are "very big" and can charge with fury.

LION

As soon as she got up, my mother hurried to my grandmother and told her: "I wandered off the track,

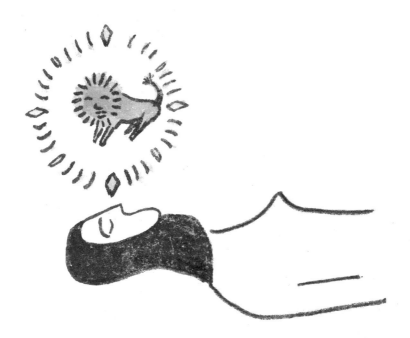

A lion is brave and ferocious. Your child will be a king of men.

139

looking for a village on the hill. To make matters worse, it was such a pitch-dark night that I couldn't even see my nose. But I continued about in search of my path.

Finally finding the light of the hamlet, I ran madly toward it. No sooner had I gotten to the entrance than something appeared in front of me. Alarmed, I knew it was a ferocious animal. He was big and strong, and his face looked like a lion's. Growling, he was coming at me.

I entered a blind alley, backing up helplessly against a wall, I shouted timidly, "Get away right now!;" but the lion snapped at my right arm. It was dripping with blood. When I looked at the running blood, I cried out, 'Oh, no!,' and woke up."

My grandmother said to her, "A lion means a boy with a progressive and triumphant character. Being bit by a lion means the boy will set the world on fire." I (the lion) am studying hard now.

(Mr. Pak, student)

A "ferocious" boy may bite the "right," *yang* "side."
Lion dreams: 88% 男.

MONKEY

One day, I was observing a big apple tree. Many large apples were on it. I approached, but some people blocked my way. "What's the matter?" I asked.

"The apple tree is being kept by the monkey, so it is impossible to come near," they replied. Despite this, I ventured up to the tree.

As I got near, the monkey suddenly threw itself into my arms, and I woke up.

A girl was born to my sister-in-law. A monkey means brilliance. My niece is a brilliant nine year old.

(Mrs. Lee, teacher)

A girl abandons herself into another's arms. Apples are also *yin*, cool and juicy.

MOUSE

The Venerable Tongjin (869-947) was a Buddhist high priest and teacher of the first three kings of the Koryŏ kingdom. Before his birth, his mother dreamt that a white rat scampered up to her, carrying a piece of blue glass in its mouth.

(Ch'a, Chŏng, and Lee, "Boy Preference")

The white mouse meant purity, and the glass the clarity of a monk's mind.

One day my mother was opening the storehouse to get a gourd full of rice, in order to prepare dinner, and she was surprised to see a crowd of mice inside.

The fortuneteller told her that her son would have good fortune, because he was born on the hour, day, month and year of the Mouse, 1960. I am obedient and shy.

(Mr. Lee, student)

Whiskered noses indicate a mousy, prosperous boy.

RABBIT

One day, my mother spotted a little white rabbit coming down to my home in Kangwon Province. There was nothing for it to eat because there was lots of snow outdoors. It was searching for something to nibble on around the barn.

Noticing this, my grandmother was surprised, and gave

141

it some food. The rabbit had big eyes, long ears and particularly white fur; but after eating heartily, it would not stay.

As soon as my mother came out of the house, he jumped up into her bosom.

After this she had a baby, me.

(Mr. Kwon, student)

A boy jumps "up" with *yang* energy, and stays "outdoors."
Rabbit dreams: 75% 女, because rabbits are soft and cuddly.

2

In 1930, my grandmother received five rabbits as a gift from someone and wanted to raise them. On her way home, when arriving at the bank of a little river, one was missing.

My father had four brothers. One of them died in the (Korean) war, in 1950. My grandmother told me this story sadly.

(Anon., student)

TIGER

My own mother-in-law, as a young bride, gazed wistfully out from the window of her cabin on Diamond (Kŭmgang) Mountain at the red lights flickering back and forth across the sands of the stream. She opened the door.

"Where are you going?," her miner husband asked, coming over to her side, and grasping her hand to restrain her....

"The villagers are dancing with torches. I'm going to join them," she defiantly replied.

"Those aren't villagers," he whispered gruffly. "Those are eyes. That's a tiger leaping back and forth!"

Such hauntingly, glowing eyes also often appear in birth dreams.

In Korean folk tales a tiger is sometimes portrayed as a big, clumsy toy for the amusement of wild rabbits. At other times he is a wise and benevolent creature, the servant of the Mountain God, who, in turn, sometimes disguises himself as a white tiger when inspecting his domain.

In reality the tiger has so impressed the Korean psyche with its awesome presence that it was adopted as the guardian animal of the country.

The key player in the Japanese takeover of Korea (1910-1945) was Japan's former Prime Minister, Itō Hirobumi, who became Resident-General, or governor over both the foreign relations and internal affairs of Korea. As an expression of Korean outrage over the loss of their independence, he was assassinated by a young man, An Chung-gŭn (1879-1910), who was executed in turn.

One day, An's father dreamed that a big tiger suddenly appeared and cried out for him to hide him. He felt pity for the tiger, so he concealed him in the storeroom. After a few minutes, a hunter hurried out of the woods, and asked, "Did you see a big tiger run by?"

"No, I didn't..."

The hunter dashed away, searching.

Then Mr. An opened the door to the storeroom. But, to his astonishment, it was empty! He kept on looking all over for the tiger. At last, he found him in his own bedroom!

Mr. An was so surprised he woke up.

A little later, he told the story to his wife. She was very glad and said, "We'll have a son as brave as a tiger."
(Mr. Cho, student)

An Chung-gŭn is still revered today in Korea.

I

My sister-in-law was looking at two big eggs in her room. Neighbors said they would turn into baby tigers.

While she was watching, they suddenly began producing a great deal of smoke. Finally one made a big noise in the smoky air. As the air cleared, a pretty, baby tiger had hatched from the egg.

She had a boy. He is five years old, and always cheerful.
(Anon., teacher)

"Smoke" and "a big noise" come from budding *yang* energy.

2

My great-aunt said, "One day, my sister and I are climbing and we discover a cave. Entering, we find three tiger cubs. I fold one into my skirt. But my sister worries very much, since taking a cub is very dangerous. It is natural for its parents to be angry at us. So, while we are returning home, I give it to her.

"One day after this dream, I received a phone call from my sister telling me she **was** pregnant. She had a very handsome son."

My uncle is brave and wild, and an architect.
(Miss Shim, student)

The destiny of child and mother is unclear until the dream drama is wholly played out.

3

My mother said, "I am living in a remote country place in a straw-roofed house. As I open the kitchen door intending to make breakfast, I see a big tiger is eating beans inside.

Surprised, I slam the door and grasp the door-handle. Trembling with fear, I am covered in sweat."

She had a daughter, me. I have a good heart, but I am indecisive.

(Anon., teacher)

A girl dwells in "the kitchen."

4

My father was feeding his cow. All of a sudden, a tiger leapt into his front yard. As the tiger glared at him, my father embraced it. To his surprise, he wasn't afraid; still, it bit his right shoulder, springing away to the backyard.

My father chased after it, but the tiger couldn't be seen. Instead, he found a big chestnut tree.

Seven months later, a son was born in my family. My father named him "Yang-ho." *Ho* means "Tiger." My brother is handsome and witty; a businessman, dealing in electrical wires.

(Mrs. To, teacher)

A boy favors the "right" side, and may bite his father, since *yangs* can disagree.

The bite makes him "witty" and "electrical."

5

My landlady had been riding to her farm in an ox-cart.

Suddenly a tiger appeared and bit the ox that had been pulling the cart. The ox disappeared, and the tiger was now drawing the cart. My landlady awoke with a start.

Ten days later her son was born.

(Mr. Hyŏn, student)

A son, being *yang*, pulls his mother.

6

My mother was searching for some medicinal herbs on a hill. As she turned around she found many kinds of flowers. As she was busy picking flowers of various colors, she didn't know that it was getting dark. She realized it only when it was completely dark, but there was no way for her to find the way home. She didn't know what to do.

She looked around and, suddenly, there was a glimmering of lights. She stared at them and saw that they were tiger's eyes. The lights came closer, but she wasn't afraid. The tiger didn't seem dangerous. She patted it on its back, and with its bright eyes, it led her home.

My brother was born. He is a kindly and helpful doctor.

(Mr. Lee, student)

A boy's eyes are "bright" with magical power.
"Herbs" and assisting her make him a doctor.

7

My mother told me, "One night I was winding along a narrow way. The moon was bright. There were many trees. Without object, I walked and walked, not knowing where I was going.

At last I was too tired to walk anymore. Then I saw a dangerous wolf. I stepped back, but another enemy was there. It was a white-haired tiger.

The wolf had me by the ear. There was nothing I could do but die. But in the twinkling of an eye, the wolf bounded away and the tiger came and knelt before me. With him, I walked until daybreak."

My mother is no longer alive, but my grandmother interprets the dream like this; "A white tiger is a sacred animal. He governs all beasts. He has dignity. You will be another tiger in this world. To be a real tiger, you must overcome all obstacles, like wolves. But I believe in your abilities."

(Mr. Chang, student)

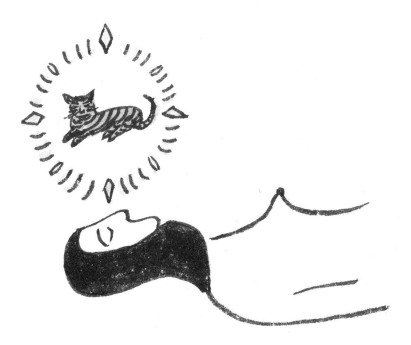

A tiger is magical, virile and courageous. Your child will be a warrior.

A boy has the courage to chase away a wolf so as to protect his mother.

8

One day my wife said to me sadly, "A tiger jumped at us. I fought with it, and as I fell down, it caught up the baby and ran away. I wept and wept with anger."

After a few months my wife suffered a miscarriage.

About two years later, my wife told me, "A big tiger was in a wild field. It crept up to me and lowered its neck. After a few minutes it disappeared."

Several months later we got a brave boy.

(Mr. Kim, teacher)

The tiger stole the baby's "spirit," then replaced it with his own. Bowing is a display of filial piety.
Tiger dreams: 81% 男.

WILDCAT

On a dark night, my mother was passing by grave mounds in the mountain. Suddenly a small wildcat sprang in front of her. She was taken aback and fled to her parents' home. However, the wildcat raced after her until she arrived at the house. And just as she was entering the gate, it leapt up and bit her middle finger.

Surprised, my mother woke up.

After a while she had a baby girl. She has grown up to be pretty, very shy, and melancholy. Difficulty in being intimate is her only weakness. She is me.

(Miss Pak, student)

A girl is "small," and may bite her mother, since two *yins* are apt to fight.

WOLF

A wolf sneaked into my house. I caught it, and tossed it over the fence to my neighbor's yard.

Both she and I were pregnant at the time. My baby miscarried, but my neighbor's child grew up to be a famous lawyer.

(Mrs. Pae, dentist's wife)

A baby's "spirit" can be tossed into another's womb (yard), via a dream.

Wolves make "good" lawyers.

BARNYARD ANIMALS

CAT

In the northern part of my hometown, there was a simple airport for the U.S. Army. Around it were a number of high school girls, dressed in white uniforms, grasping lilies in their hands. I was observing the scene from a high cliff.

Meanwhile, a little cat was climbing up to me along the cliff. Surprised, I tried knocking it back down into a stream, but it wouldn't give up. With the cat climbing ceaselessly up to me, I couldn't stand it any more. Astonished, I woke up.

Afterwards, my daughter was born. Girl students, lilies and a cat mean a baby girl.

(Mrs. Yu, teacher)

"Little" is a girl. A "cliff" symbolizes the female organ.

CHICKEN

1

People dressed in white were going to a little hut in the forest. One of them was carrying a strange box in his arms. Curious about the contents of the box, my mother asked for it, but he would not give it to her.

She asked persistently and, at last, they were fighting. She won and took the odd box back home. As soon as she opened it, a beautiful cock sprang from it. The crowing of the cock was loud and brave.

My mother gave birth to a baby boy. Perhaps the people in white are my ancestors.

(Mr. Son, student)

A boy becomes a "cock," who crows "loud and brave."
Rooster dreams: 86% 男.

This dream was influenced by a myth in the *Samguk Yusa* that a baby, the forefather of the Kim family of Shilla, was found in a box in the forest by where a golden cock was crowing.

2

An old hen appeared, while Grandmother (then twenty two years old) was bathing in a stream, and said, "I will give you one of my feathers, but don't lose it; " and warned, "If you do, your baby will suffer misfortune."

Just then, Grandmother dropped the feather in the stream.

Very sad, she confessed the dream to her family. Her husband scolded her for being superstitious. She has tried to sleep, dreaming in search of the fallen feather every night, but has failed to find it so far. She is still trying, though she is in her sixties.

My mother was a frail baby and still is weak.
(Miss Won, student)

A girl becomes a "hen."
Hen (and "chicken") dreams: 71% 女.

COW

My father-in-law was watching a cow without a bridle.
She had red hair and sharp horns. Her eyes were shining
like flames. Their brightness was so intense that he could
not look straight at her. Her moo was like the roaring of
thunder. She dashed to the east as fleet as a sailing ship.
It was so fascinating that he could never forget it.

A boy was born. He is very creative, and working as a
computer systems engineer.
(Anon., teacher)

"Sharp horns," flaming eyes, etc., change "her" *yin* into "his"
yang.
Cow (including "calf," "bull" and "ox") dreams: 80% 男.

DOG

My mother was threading her way through a field of
ripe grain. While walking, she found a house which was
covered with gourds, and she stepped indoors. Inside,
there was an elderly man and many kinds of fruit. When
she left, he gave her two white puppies.

She took them in her arms and continued on her way.
When she looked back to see the house again, it was
gone. The puppies had gone away, too. Then the field
turned into the sea and she yearned for them.

In the middle of the sea, two little girls were standing.
They were walking on the water, coming to her.

She gave birth to my elder sister, and then me. My sister is two years older than I.

(Miss Song, teacher)

The puppies were transformed into pure-hearted girls, though one had to wait two more years (in Limbo?) before being conceived.

GOAT

My grandmother was walking through some fields in the middle of the night, and was passing a ravine. There, she spied a goat climbing up the mountain. She rushed over and caught it in her arms.

Still, she noticed yet another goat far ahead of it, and trailed it through the ravine towards the mountain until she caught it and lifted it up in her arms. She returned home, overjoyed, with two lustrous black (native) goats.

My aunt and my mother each gave birth to baby boys a half year later. I like company, but also solitude.

(Anon., student)

Boys are "lustrous," and climb "up" on their way out of the darkness of *yin*.

HORSE

I

My mother said, "It had been raining day after day until the whole village was filled with water. As if someone had been pouring water from the sky, it was such a big shower. Finally the whole earth was covered with water, except for my house.

A deep blue sea was all over. In fear of death, I prayed to *Shillyŏngnim* (a god) from my heart, in the back of my house. In answer to my prayer, the rain stopped. Bird-shaped clouds appeared all over the sky. All of a sudden, a white horse with a knight mounted on it, charged out of the clouds, and pranced into my bosom.

So I thought it was going to be a son. But I had a daughter, you."

I am calm and kind, altruistic, but a little obstinate.
(Anon., teacher)

A flood signifies feminine waters.
The "white horse" makes her good-hearted, but the "knight," a bit "obstinate."

2

Suddenly my aunt was in a sandy desert. Of course, she didn't know where she was. There was no one and nothing nearby. The sun blazed intensely. Thirsty, she sought water. She was wandering around the desert, but a bit later found an oasis. Pleased, she ran there.

There, she saw two white horses drinking water, and a coach nearby. Inside the coach was something that looked like a baby. She approached to look more closely, but her husband woke her up.

Six months later she had twin sons. They are in kindergarten, very cute and gentle as lambs.
(Miss Cho, student)

A blazing "desert," and "thirst" signify masculine fire.
Horse dreams: 71% 男.

PIG

In the Orient, a pig is considered a sign of vigor and prosperity.

During the reign of Wu-ti (140–87 B.C.), the "Celestial Empire" of the Han dynasty of China reached its peak. Wu-ti instituted many successful agricultural and social reforms. His father (an emperor too) dreamt that he saw a very big, red pig (the color of a fiery sun) entering one of his several houses.

The man hurried to the house and glancing up, noticed that the sky was full of red clouds. The clouds descended and cloaked the house, and amidst the red glow he made out a long dragon. After resting a while it suddenly rose up into the sky.

The emperor asked a diviner the meaning of this dream, and was told that, "You will have a son in that house."

Then the emperor told his favorite wife to move there. She obeyed, and while residing therein dreamt an angel offered her the sun and she ate it.

A few days later she realized she was pregnant, and after fourteen months gave birth to a boy, the future Wu-ti.

(Mrs. Wang Su-yi, professor)

The different stages of this dream point out various aspects of Wu-ti's life. A "pig" indicates prosperity. "Red" and "sun" show heavenly blessings. And the dragon rising to the sky symbolizes becoming emperor.

A possibly related story arose in Korea, 300 years later. In the *Samguk Sagi* (History of the Three Kingdoms), it says: Sansang, the king of Koguryŏ (196–227 A.D.), was praying on top of a mountain to a heaven god for an heir.

One night, in his sleep, he heard an earth-shaking voice saying, "Don't worry, you will have a son by your second wife." He woke up, wondering at this, for he only had one

An angel has brought you a child. It will be pretty, holy and magical.

wife, the queen.

One day, a pig escaped from the palace courtyard. Though the cooks chased after it, nobody but a pretty, village girl could catch it. The king, hearing of this talented, healthy girl, visited her in the night, saying, "I am the king, won't you sleep with me?"

Honored, she replied, "Yes, but if I bear your child, please don't let it be hurt by the (jealous) queen."

"I promise; I won't." And she bore him an heir, Tong-ch'ŏn (ruled 227-248), in accordance with the dream.

One can suppose, after hearing such an impressive voice, that the king had been keeping an eye open for "a second wife." When she caught the pig, it was his "son."

I

About forty years ago, my maternal grandmother was living in a Korean-style house in Suwon, and had a large field. In summer, she ordered her servant to sow Chinese cabbage seeds, and the cabbages flourished.

One day, she strode from her garden to the field. Upon arriving, she intended to pick some cabbages to pickle into *kimch'i*. Suddenly a huge black (native) pig appeared, laying its belly down on the cabbage field, and began to eat cabbages.

My grandmother passed her hand gently over the pig's

A mother pig is generous and abundant. Your baby will be rich and bear many children.

back. She wasn't surprised by the pig. On the contrary, she brought it along home with her.

She became pregnant with my uncle. Quick-tempered and ambitious, he is the head of a department for a company.

(Miss Kim, student)

A son is "huge."
Pig dreams : 76% 男

2

My mother dreamt, "Many wild animals were chasing after me and I ran away very fast so as not to be caught. After running for a long time, I found a shabby house and old woman living in it. She gave me a small pig, and said, 'If you take this pig and go over there (she gestured) you will find a river. Go across it and you will be safe.'

I wrapped the pig up in my skirt and then waded across the river. As she said, I was safe."

She had a girl, me. I am shy, and responsible.

(Miss Pak, teacher)

"Small" is *yin*, a daughter.
She was placed in her mother's womb (skirt); and the river crossed was life. The other animals maybe were "spirits" wishing to enter her womb.

SHEEP

My wife was alone gazing at the sky. Many stars were shining brightly. All of a sudden, she saw a pair of lambs on one side of the sky, flying to the other side. The path of flight was semi-circular, like a rainbow.

After the lambs, a pair of cows and a couple of pigeons flew along the same path.

157

We had a girl. In infancy, she cried a lot and was slightly irritable, but now she isn't. She is a little shy, but intelligent, and attending kindergarten.

(Anon., teacher)

Pairs of girls play at night along a "rainbow" path; the number two is *yin*.

Part Four

DREAMS OF GODS AND HUMANS

Village babies are being born and carried about on the backs of their mothers all the time and kids are playing everywhere one turns. Adoration for the children of others will someday attract a baby's "spirit" to a young woman's dreams.

Folks do not know where babies "come from," so they make up stories, such as, "Gods give (the secret of) life to human beings." Thus women pray to and dream of gods as a prelude to pregnancy.

Such a misty world it was.
Down the aisle a woman in white was
passing between lines of cribs. Across the long
room, she was coming to me, I knew.
Her hands reached in to pick me up. I was
afraid. Picking me up, she could feel my fear.
She let go, laying me back on the mattress.
Clouds rippled away from her cap and
apron.
All around me were white clouds.
I found myself alive in a body, in a place I didn't
know. I had forgotten how I came there,
where I'd lived before, or if I'd ever lived at
all....

CHILDREN

Kangsu was a Confucian scholar (?-692) in the Shilla kingdom, who argued for the adoption by the State of moral principles which could be applied to worldly affairs, as opposed to the "other-worldly" view of Buddhism. His mother saw a baby in a dream, but a horn was sticking out of his head.
(Mr. Kang, student)

Professor Rhi Bou-young says, "The horn is an animal charac teristic and shows the holiness of the child."

BABY BOY

A woman dreamt of a smiling baby, who was clasping two white balls of unequal size in his hands. By chance, the bigger one fell and though he tried very hard, the baby couldn't get it back again.

The child born was a boy. He has a strong will. From childhood he had been good at both baseball and soccer, but he injured his right foot while playing soccer in high school, so he decided to become a baseball player. Indeed, he is now a famous pitcher for a popular professional, baseball team.

(Mr. Shin, teacher)

The "big" ball was for soccer.

BOYS IN VARIOUS PLACES

I

One afternoon in late autumn my sister was strolling with her husband. The street was dreary, but maple trees were still showing off gorgeous red leaves. After a while, she discovered a baby who was playing with doves. She bent over and asked, "Why are you playing so late in the night?"

The baby said, "I'm your son. Why don't you know I am your son?"

My sister was very surprised. She thought, "There are many strange things in this world," but she was happy.

She had a boy with the character of a dove. He is one

162

year old and likes everything.
(Mr. Kim, student)

2

I was climbing a tree, clasping a little boy in my arms. When I reached the top of the tree, I looked down. My younger sister was standing underneath, spreading out her long skirt. Losing my senses for a moment, I dropped my baby into my sister's skirt.

After that, my sister bore a son, but I had a daughter. It seemed as if my sister had stolen my son. My daughter is clever and bright, in the third grade.
(Anon., teacher)

3

I was near a fantastically misty pond and wanted to take a bath; so I took off my clothes and got in. While I was washing, a man approached me. He was carrying two children. One was a girl, the other a boy. But they suddenly disappeared.

Time passed. He appeared near the pond again, holding the same two children. The boy had bright eyes. I gazed into his eyes. Giving me the boy, the man departed with the girl.

I woke up remembering the boy's starry eyes.

I had a boy. He is a shy, elementary school student.
(Mrs. Kim, teacher)

4

One day, my aunt walked to a stream near the house to do her washing. While she was washing, a big peach drifted by in the water. She was very fond of peaches, so she tried catching it. She found a stick and pulled out the peach. It was good to look at and bigger than an ordinary one. She thought herself fortunate.

Dying to eat it, she tried cutting it with a knife. Suddenly the peach split open by itself, and there was a strong light in it. She was horrified and lost consciousness. When she came to her senses, there was a child's cry. The child was crying in the peach, and was a boy. He was emitting light and was very cute, like a prince in a fairy tale.

She thought that this child was from heaven and revered him. She was sure God had given him to her and that he would become a great man. She made up her mind to raise him and took him to her house.

The boy is brilliant, a student at Seoul National University.

(Anon., teacher)

A boy floats, and emits "strong light."

PURE GIRLS

I

My mother was walking along a shady road in the green mountains, and suddenly found a white house. The house was made of cookies and other delicious sweets. Attracted by the sweet smell, she entered the house. It was very clean, and a beautiful girl was silently sitting on the floor there.

My mother asked her, "What is your name? Who are your parents?" The girl was very quiet and didn't say a word.

My mother drank a glass of orange juice which was on a low table. As soon as she did this, she fell asleep.

Later, I was born.

(Miss No, student)

A daughter stays in the house, and is "sweet."

2

My mother dreamt that she and my father were walking along a road. A very bright moon approached and then retreated from them several times. Suddenly something was shining so brightly they couldn't see, or even open their eyes. Yet, they had to open their eyes to look at it, because they were told to do so by someone uttering a piercing cry.

When they went over and examined it carefully, it turned out to be the light of a candle being held up in a

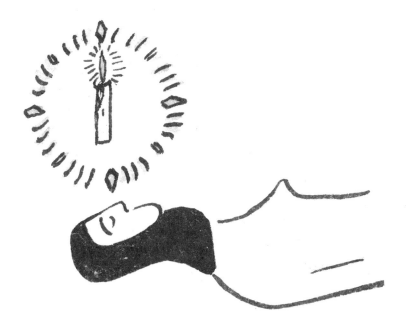

A candle is bright. Your child will be an inspired leader, lightening up the darkness of your days.

naked child's hand.

After this, my mother gave birth to my eldest sister. She is optimistic and emotional. When she was a child, she danced very well. She was loved by everybody. As she grew up she became interested in art. So she studies textiles in school.

(Anon., teacher)

A girl "retreats," and her cry is "piercing."
A candle is for optimism.

TWINS

A boy and a girl were playing on rope swings hanging from a tree-limb near my house, where I was making soya sauce. I was very glad to see them, and invited them into my house.

They said, "We should be going back home, now." But I wouldn't let them go.

I gave birth to twins, a boy and a girl. They look just like the children in the dream.

(Woman met at a Buddhist temple)

They could be waiting for a chance to escape.

TRIPLETS

My best friend's mother was lingering in an apple orchard when she saw some little boys stealing apples. The master of the orchard angrily appeared and scolded them.

The first boy was afraid and felt threatened by him. The second boy peered into the master's face, and the third boy turned away, concealing himself behind the oldest. In such ways as character and height, they differed from each other.

Surprisingly enough, his mother gave birth to three sons (triplets), and their heights differ, just as in the dream. Gradually their characters appeared. The first boy seems cowardly. The second boy challenges others to debate. The third is pessimistic.

(Mr. Chu, student)

Their life's drama was played out even before they were born.

ADULTS

Yi Sun-shin (1545-1598) invented the iron-clad turtle-boat, and became the Korean admiral, who, in a series of brilliant naval battles, successfully defeated the invading Japanese fleet of Shogun Hideyoshi Toyotomi.

Before giving birth, Yi's mother dreamt that she saw light pouring down from the sky onto a mountain. On the mountain a young man was supporting a tree, which was tottering to one side.

The light meant a great man would be born. The tree leaning to one side warned of the possible fall of the Yi dynasty. Supporting the tree, however, augured that the dynasty would be saved by the young man, as it was.

(Mr. Sŏk, student)

A Korean rarely sees her grown child, like this, in a birth dream.

AMOUR

I dreamed I was making love with Samson. While in labor I had the same dream again, and gave birth to one of my sons.

Somebody told me that if I had the same dream a third time the boy would be a great success, but I didn't have it again. My son is an architectural engineer. He looks like Samson, tall and healthy.

I told my husband, "If I did this in real life, you could chase me out, but if it's a dream, how can you be angry?"

(Woman met at a Buddhist temple)

DEPARTED RELATIVE

During the Ming dynasty (1368-1644) in China, a, now, anonymous official dreamt of a big ship sailing along a river. On the ship, two men were sitting quietly by a coffin.

A diviner told the dreamer, "You will have two sons." He did.

(Mrs. Wang Su-yi, professor)

The coffin was for the dreaming father, being carried to his funeral by the spirits of his yet, unborn children.

One night, my mother's elder sister (who had died one year before I was born) floated into my house bringing something wrapped up in a handkerchief. My mother was surprised and said, "Why have you come here at this time?"

She said, "I came to give you the present that you want most. But, don't open it before I go."

My mother wanted to talk with her more, but she said, "There is someone waiting for me, so I have to go now. And you don't have to see me off." So she hurried to go away.

My mother shouted out her name, trying to catch her, but she couldn't follow her anymore.

After this, my mother found that she was with child, and had me, a daughter.

Because of this story, I realized that "death and birth are in between a piece of paper," as they say in Buddhism. In Buddhism, all types of life transmigrate. Therefore the spirit of my aunt might have gone to heaven and sent another spirit to my mother instead. I think the universe is full of wonders.

(Miss Pang, teacher)

Koreans who practice shamanism or Buddhism tend to believe in reincarnation. Although followers of these faiths are declining and make up only about half of the present population, unconscious memories of ancestral beliefs in the transmigration of souls may still be motivating spirits for the majority of birth dreams.

GODS AND OTHERS

How vast is God
The ruler of men below!
...Heaven gave birth to the multitudes of the people...

(The Book of Poetry, Legge trs.)

Sometimes, when I am wandering around the Korean countryside, particularly in the mountains, I see women bowing before waterfalls, old birch trees and phallic or vulvar-shaped stones.

I have listened to them chanting for long hours. I have known them to kneel before portraits of the Seven Stars (Big Dipper) Spirit *Ch'ilsŏng* or else the Mountain God *Sanshin,* or even an image of Buddha to show their sincerity and to win favor, so as to be blessed with a baby, usually a son to keep up the "family lineage," or to "depend on in old age," or to perform "ancestor worship ceremonies." (Daughters are desired for docility, cuddliness, and as companions for sons.)

Some women keep praying day after day, often for "100 (meaning perfection) days," until they have a dream from, or even of the god to whom they have been praying.

They may hear the "gong" of a temple bell in a dream, being Buddha's voice, or the growl of the tiger servant of the Mountain God, helping their dreams come true.

Or they might hear the words of a god: Professor Oh Han-jin of my university told me, "My mother was already thirty seven years old, but hadn't had any sons. One night she dreamed that an old man came up to her and said, 'If you want to have a son, you must move to Seoul.' She was living in the country but, deciding to follow the advice of the dream grandfather, she moved with her husband to Seoul.

"Soon after arriving in Seoul, she had another dream: A shepherd came up to her, and asked, 'Why are you sighing so; what is troubling you?'

She looked up at him and said, 'I have no son.'

He replied, 'What if I become your son?'

She looked at him, and then beyond into the distance. Far away in the haze, another figure was standing, but she couldn't see it clearly.

Ten months after this dream, I, her son, was born. My name, 'Han-jin,' means 'Stay in Seoul.'

Now I am the shepherd of my family. The vague figure was my younger sister."

During the winter of 1985, while in Miari, a district of Seoul, I was visiting some blind fortunetellers, who live in a colony of white, blue-tiled houses, and asked them about birth dreams.

One plucky woman of about fifty, in a traditional,

green dress (*hanbok*), rolled her empty eyes, telling me, "A *t'aemong* (birth dream) can occur at any time, but when a woman has many pregnancy dreams, the first one dreamed is the *t'aemong*. If a woman has many dreams and just chooses the one she likes, it is not good.

"There are three gods inside a person: Heaven god, Earth god and Man god (*'Ch'ŏn'*, *'Chi'* and *'In-shin'*). The three gods make the person dream. The three gods together. Because a person believes in the gods, they are always concerned about him. As a person lets others know when something has happened, so gods let a person know what will happen. People can't see the gods. The gods only show them the images in dreams.

"The Heaven and Earth gods make the Man god walk in dreams. The gods make the mother dream, and they show an image in a dream. The image is the Man god of the new child."

This was intriguing to me. "Man god of the new child!" I whispered. Could it exist independently of the mother and enter, like a spirit, into her dreams? But again, an embryo has its own spark of life; where did it come from?

"Are dreams composed of spirits?" I inquired.

The blind lady turned her eyes toward me—they were like swirling clouds.... "Of course, one dreams in the world seen by the spirit while the body is sleeping.

"The Heaven god and Earth god are spirits too. They help people and direct them. The Heaven god is like a father; the Earth god like a mother. They work together as a family.

"When people die, their spirits go to the Heaven god. The Heaven god makes them reborn in the world. Human beings continue coming into this world, dying and being reborn. The Heaven and Earth gods decide how one will be reborn. Past relationships and *karma* (deeds) affect this. If you had an unfinished relationship with someone in a past life, when reborn you can meet again."

BIRTH GRANDMOTHER

A variety of gods, due to the Korean traditions of shamanism, Taoism, Buddhism and Christianity, give people babies, but an intermediary, the white-haired *Samshin Halmŏni* ("Womb-spirit" Grandmother), delivers the baby's spirit to the womb. She sometimes appears in dreams with a gift, like a piece of fruit or a fish, symbolizing the sex of the newly conceived baby.

Mrs. Jang Doe-her, a lively grandmother from a southern, Chŏlla province village, told me, "Our ancestor, *Chiwang*, goes to the mountain and carries the baby's spirit down from the place of the mountain spirits. She brings the baby to the womb and cares for it until forty nine days after its birth. After forty nine days, she leaves for 'the other world.'

It is the Mountain God who gives a great beast (like a tiger) to a mother; the *Chiwang* is only the carrier of the child's spirit, like a stork."

Mr. Lee Jae-hyung, an eighty year old friend, gave me a Seoul version: "The *Samshin* is the baby's god. The baby's god protects the baby until 100 days after birth. One or two months before birth, she appears in the mother's dream. She foretells that you will have a baby. Then she appears again, not long after the baby is born. She appears four or five times during pregnancy, and four or five times after pregnancy in dreams. Everyone prays to her to protect the baby.

"A father's *Samshin* passes on to his son. A son's *Samshin* passes on to the grandson. So each house has a different *Samshin*.

The Samshin Halmŏni (*the Birth Grandmother*) *appears in a dream, carrying a fish, the spirit symbol of a baby, to its mother's womb.*

"Fifty years ago, people used to pray to the *Samshin* for a baby, and then go to the mountain and pray to the Mountain God, or go to the Buddhist temple and pray there. The Mountain God decides the baby's spirit, or else Buddha does. The Mountain God or Buddha decides its fortune and its sex, too. The *Samshin* takes care of the baby's health and life.

"If one has a dream of Buddha, that is the *Samshin* in disguise. If the dream is of the Mountain God, that is her, too."

She also appears as herself:

My mother dreamed she was wandering about a mountain covered with chestnut trees. Under the trees many ripe chestnuts were scattered about. She had a gourd, and filled it up with chestnuts.

Then an elderly, white-haired woman—we call her, *"Samshin* Grandmother," came out of the trees. She said, "No one can come to this mountain and pick chestnuts without my leave." She snatched the gourd of chestnuts from my mother. My mother clung to the woman, crying and begging, and said, "I picked them; they are mine! They are mine! Please give them back! Please!"

After a while the elderly woman said, "I was moved by your sincerity. I will give them back to you." My mother got the gourd back. From it she grasped the five biggest, ripest chestnuts, and woke up.

I, a girl, was born.
(Miss Lee, student)

A girl is "ripe," a faithful girl; but a hollow "gourd," called a *pagaji,* implies a gossip.

BUDDHA

Prince Regent Shotoku-taishi (573-621) was a champion of Buddhism in Japan, advocating it as a religion for the salvation of all social classes. Before his conception, his mother, a princess, saw a monk dressed in gold coming towards her in a dream. He said, "I have taken an oath to save the world. Momentarily, I wish to take shelter in your womb..."

The lady replied, "My womb isn't pure. How can you find shelter in it?"

The monk declared, "I don't fear impurity;" and it seemed to the lady that he entered her mouth with one bound, and she awoke from her dream.

After this she conceived, and bore the prince.

(Adapted from *The World of Dreams*, by Ralph L. Woods)

Buddha has given you a child. Unselfish and compassionate, one day, it will give itself back to Buddha.

1

On a pleasant spring day, my mother and some friends went on a picnic near a royal tomb. There was a small Buddhist temple nearby.

While her friends played, my mother crept alone into the sermon hall and stole a small image of Buddha. She came back home with it.

The dream recurred and she became pregnant.

I was born five months later. My mother was a bit disappointed to have a daughter. I am warm-hearted and sensitive.

(Miss Sang, student)

"Small" is for a girl Buddha.
Theft, even in a dream, doesn't always turn out as one plans.

2

My wife was climbing up T'oham Mountain. The famous stone cave, Sŏkkuram (built in the Shilla period about 1,000 years ago), was covered with snow. The trees were also covered. Suddenly while she was climbing, a gray haired, Buddhist monk appeared, and said, "Follow me." So she walked along the mountain path with him. On both sides of the path, many stone images of Buddha greeted them. While she was wondering at this, the monk disappeared, and she lost her path in a cave. It was cool and dark inside.

After a while she flew up into the sky, which was as high and still. All sad sounds of the world fell asleep. Suddenly a strong wind blew up, and my wife awoke.

The dream was on March 20, 1966. On December 10, 1966, my eldest son was born.

(Mr. Cho, teacher)

A monk has blessed your baby, and he will guide it to an understanding of its original nature.

A monk implies a pious boy; gray hair gives him long life.

CHRIST

My husband and I were polishing a life-size statue of Christ so as to suspend him from a wooden Cross. The color of the Cross changed and Christ was brought to life. Rising up and smiling, he asked my husband to shake hands.

My husband was afraid of shaking hands.

We had a bright girl.

(Anon., teacher)

177

Christ and the Cross inspire a devout child, regardless of sex.

There are other Christian-style birth dreams, usually set in a church. The dreamer arranges flowers, plays the piano, or even catches pumpkins rolling down from the altar. Children of such dreams are believed to be especially blessed by God.

CONFUCIUS

Yi Hwang (T'oegye) (1501–1570) was a distinguished Korean, Neo-Confucian philosopher. He emphasized that one's personal inner experience and moral self-cultivation were the bases of learning. Before his birth his mother dreamt that she was walking through the open wooden gates of a Confucian shrine.

Years later, on the day her son graduated from a Confucian academy, a white cloud appeared over the roof of her house and it began to snow.

(Un-gae Pillow)

1

Mother saw Confucius teaching the Classical Canon.

I was conceived. My name, *Wal* means "Words," and *Kyo* means "Teach." I'd like to be a teacher, so I am studying hard.

(Mr. Yi, student)

Confucius fosters a scholarly child and appeals, primarily, to males.

2

It was cloudy. Suddenly, a bright light appeared in the sky. My wife climbed up towards the spot and a clean dale appeared. The view was fantastic. She descended along a valley for some time, until coming to a big bower.

There, a scholar in white, wearing a Korean (black, broad-rimmed) hat, was studying. A colorful stone tortoise was in front of the bower.

We had a daughter.

When she was four years old she could read fairy tales, write and keep a diary. She was so strong she could climb up on the Ulsan Rock of Sŏrak Mountain by herself. She plays the piano, is artistic, and outgoing.

(Mr. Kim, teacher)

"A valley" has a feminine atmosphere. A girl is also "colorful." The "scholar" gives her reading and writing. Color is for art. "Stone tortoise," for strength.

A Confucian classic says your child will be a right-minded scholar.

GODDESS

My mother told me, "I seemed to be suspended from some kind of filament, and a goddess was hovering in the midst of light and shadows. One end of the thread was, somehow, inside me, and the other was high up in shadows. Circling around me were eyes, mysterious eyes.

Suddenly the goddess gave me something and whispered in a sweet voice, 'This is a valuable purple cloth that can never be found in the secular city. Take good care of it.' She looked at me—really looked at me, and smiled.

She said, 'Alright, it's time to go, but don't forget what I told you.' And she took my hand. Suddenly the air was sweet, the ground began to shake, and I could feel something powerful inside me."

This dream was vivid and recurrent.

After ten months, I could see the wonderful world filled with so many beautiful flowers and birds. I think the purple cloth the goddess gave to my mother is me, and I have come to believe that I am from another universe. Perhaps I may have been a prince with a sad fate. Now, I think of myself as a prince, living a life of mercy and dignity.

(Mr. Kim, student)

"Purple" is a noble color.
"Something powerful" is a boy.

KING OF HEAVEN

One day, my mother had a vision of the god of Taoism *(Ok'wang Sangje)*, who rules the universe. She thought it odd.

At once she began preparing a ceremony. Wanting to get rid of sickness and worry, she prepared food and drink with all her heart. When the ceremony began, the god scoffed at the food on the table and was very angry. He said, "How poor it is!"

The god leapt down to earth from his palace and was searching for a stick to beat her with. She was very surprised at this and ran away, hiding in a corner of her house.

She woke up.

The child was my brother. He is shy and prudent. He owns a small factory for making bags.

(Anon., teacher)

2

My mother met a monk who was knocking nuts from a big tree with a stick. She came up to him and said, "Venerable monk, please give me some nuts." He gave her a handful of small ones.

My mother said to him, "Oh, no, Venerable monk, I don't want many nuts, please give me just one big nut. I want a big one." Then choosing a nut from the tree, he gave it to her.

She held it with her two hands. It became three nuts. They were very big, bright and dark brown. My mother thanked him, grasping them in her hands and kept on going.

At last she arrived at a mountain. Many people were standing in a line. The King of Heaven was at the center and many subjects were standing around him. He said to my mother, "For what are you living in this world?"

She answered unhesitatingly, "My children come first.

I only live for my children."

He said, "Oh, you are a wonderful woman. Your sacrifice will be rewarded. Let the band play for her!" As he finished his words, a beautiful song was played for my mother.

She was very happy, grasping the three nuts in her hands again.

I think my mother's birth dream came true, because I have one brother and sister. We are three in all. My father died when I was eight years old, so my mother had difficulty raising us. I think that she is really a sacrificing woman.

(Mrs. Lee, teacher)

MOUNTAIN GOD

I

As I was tramping through the woods, all of a sudden the God of Mountains (*Sanshin*) appeared before me with a baby in his arms. He said, "This baby is being chased by a fox. I'm going to give him to you. You'd better take him along and hide him."

So I took the baby, setting out for home with him in haste. As soon as I arrived at my house, I entered the inner room, and concealed myself under the covers with the baby.

About nine months later, I gave birth to the boy whom the god had given me.

(Anon., teacher)

In a folk tale, a fox (with nine tails) changed into a pretty witch who preyed on young men.

From a peak up in the sky, the Mountain God sends down gifts of babies in answer to the prayers, of lonely, but faithful women.

2

My mother was staring at a big peach tree. It was very thick with green leaves.

On the tree was a spirit with a wooden stick, long white hair and a beard. He had a large peach in his hands and gave it to my mother.

My sister was born.

She has self-respect, and is a housewife.

(Anon., teacher)

"Green leaves," along with the flower, are soft *yin* parts of a plant.

OLD MAN IN WHITE

I

In my mother's dream, three or four old men with white hair and beards were lying on the grass of a small island in the middle of a river. Over the river was a stone bridge. My mother and I were passing by the white-haired men, who were smiling brightly.

My mother happened to see a baby beside them. It was splashing into the knee-deep water. "It's dangerous!," she shrieked, and rushed to the baby. Unexpectedly it smiled

A wise, old man has given you a baby, and he will guard it closely as it grows up.

184

and held out its hands. So my mother embraced it, and hurried me across the bridge.

The old men were still resting and smiling at us. We could see the baby was a boy, for it was naked.

He is wise and handsome. My mother still believes my son is protected by gods, those old men.

(Anon., teacher)

Such men may be ancestors, or else *Shinsŏn* who become "gods" through perfection of spiritual practices.

PRESIDENT AND FIRST LADY

I

One day, all the people who lived in our town were ordered by the president (probably Rhęe Syng-man) to come to the beach (Youngil Gulf on the east coast). So my mother went, too.

The president said, "A jewel box, decorated with pearls and diamonds is falling from the sky, and anyone who catches it should bring it to me." So all the people peered up at the sky. A half hour later, the jewel box appeared in the sky and fell slowly towards my mother's skirt. A few minutes later, she caught it, and opened it. There was a picture of the president in the box. So she shouted loudly, and woke up.

I am the cheerful daughter born of this dream.

(Mrs. Kim, teacher)

A "jewel box" is a *yin* container, and so belongs to a girl.

The dream suggests that some people, deep inside, still believe children come from "the sky."

2

The First Lady, Mrs. Yuk (wife of President Park Chung-hee), was visiting my parents' house. Her face was very beautiful and her hair was made up. Her figure was very graceful. I was honored and happy that she was visiting my house.

She walked to my spacious yard. The yard was full of many people and we had a big party for her. I held her hand, wandering along the bank of a stream. I talked about my father, who had been on the Board of Education.

Ten months later I had a daughter. She is pretty and clever, and the best student in her fifth grade class. She can play the piano very well, and is good at cleaning the house.

(Mrs. Yun, teacher)

A First Lady encourages a second. Mrs. Yuk was a virtuous woman dedicated to the society.

SANTA CLAUS

My mother was visiting her friend's house, one day, spending a few hours with her. When returning home, she felt hungry, so she went to the kitchen to eat lunch. She was surprised to find a big bag in the kitchen. She didn't know whose it was. She wanted to know who had brought the bag and what it contained, so she asked some neighbors about it.

One of them said, "I saw Santa Claus carrying a big bag on his back. He entered your kitchen and put it down there."

My mother asked again, "Why did he do that?"

"Because he wanted to give you a present for Christmas. He said so, of course," her friend answered.

My mother immediately opened the bag and found many socks, toys, books, and a big clock. She picked the clock up out of the bag and hung it on the wall. She was happy to look at it. After a few minutes, the pendulum began swinging. Soon, she could hear the clock striking loudly, and woke up.

I was born. I am an honest and friendly, though impatient man; a good teacher.

(Mr. Hwang)

A clock's "pendulum" tells it is time for a son.

Part Five

DREAM TREASURES

Babies are regarded as treasures: "a gem," "a pearl," "silver" and "gold," and other precious objects. When the stirrings of life are intuitively detected in a woman's womb, such a "precious one" glitters in her dreams.

A lady was pregnant, but a widow, because her husband had died in battle. She was living in a small cottage.

One night, she dreamed she saw a big star suddenly falling. She could not look up at it because it was so luminous.

Meanwhile, she heard an old man's voice saying, "I'm going to give you a present. This shiny stone. If you swallow it, you will have a son and he will be a great man."

Upon hearing this, she turned to the old man, who was beside her, took the stone from him, and swallowed it with one gulp.

A few days later she gave birth to Chang Yŏng-shil, a gifted, Korean scientist and astronomer during the reign of King Sejong (1418–1450).

JEWELS

SCATTERED JEWELS

I

My mother was visiting her next-door neighbor. The neighbor stepped into the kitchen to fix a treat.

While her host was in the kitchen, my mother suddenly decided to open the drawers and began rifling through them.

One was full of pearls, diamonds and other precious stones. Shining in the drawer they were very beautiful. She stole all of them and returned to her house.

Maybe they mean me, her daughter. I am grown up, but not very beautiful.

  (Miss Kim, student)

A drawer is a *yin* receptacle, and thus a place for a girl.
Beauty can not be stolen; and her mother would never be quite at ease with what she has done.

2

As my mother was gazing at the sky, many stars were twinkling. Suddenly they fell on her. Surprised, she raised her hand, and many stars fell into it, too.

Looking at her hand, she was surprised again because of the stars.

The twinkling stars began changing into glittering jewels, like sapphires or diamonds in her hand. Pleased, she cried out to the sky, and awoke.

When I see stars I feel good about my future. My mother says, "You will be rich because of the jewels."

  (Mr. Yang, student)

3

I was walking in the middle of the night along a mountain path and could barely see. Then, before me appeared a tiger pit with pine branches laid over it and I carefully edged by so as not to fall in. While doing so, I noticed some light pouring through the cracks between the pine needles, but I kept on going up the path.

Finally, curious, I paused and returned to the glowing pit, peering in. To my surprise there was a very big diamond at the bottom. It was so bright that I couldn't look at it directly. Quickly I scrambled down into the pit and embraced it.

Then I climbed out and started on my way back up the mountain, but as I glanced around I saw many dark figures coming out of the forest, chasing after me. They were trying to take away the diamond, so I ran as fast I could to the clay wall of a thatched hut, jumped over it, and got safely inside the hut.

I had a son, whose face shines bright like a diamond. (Anon., secretary)

One, "very big" and "so bright," are all signs of *yang*.
The dark figures are probably jealous "spirits."
Jewel dreams: 67% 女.

BEAD

My grandmother was strolling along the seashore. It was wavy and foggy. Suddenly a small island arose in the middle of the sea. On the island was an old man with a long white beard. My grandmother was surprised and confused. The old man told her, "I want to give you this present, come here."

She said, "I can't, because I don't have a boat."

He said, "Open your long skirts."

She did, and he threw a single bead to her. It was pure blue.

Other women gathered around her. They wanted to see the bead. She gripped it and didn't show it to anyone.

She returned home and opened her palm. It was stained blue.

My mother was born. She grew up to be bright and beautiful.

(Miss Cho, student)

A blue bead (of *yin* water) is feminine; a red one (of *yang* fire), masculine.

PEARL

Hsu Chen-chun, "the dragon-slayer," was a Chinese, Taoist magician born in 239. "His mother became pregnant after dreaming that a golden-plumaged phoenix let a pearl drop from its beak into her womb."

"During times of drought (Hsu) had only to touch a piece of tile to turn it into gold, and thus relieve the people of their distress."

(E.T.C. Werner, *A Dictionary of Chinese Mythology*)

I

My mother was tired from working, and dreamed of the paradise of her childhood. The long golden beaches and white sand beaches, so white they hurt her eyes. And the high mountains and great, brown highlands of beautiful colors. She was living along that coast every day and night.

In her dreams, she saw beautiful girls and handsome boys holding many flowers, and heard the surf roaring. Someone came to her riding in a boat. His clothes were bright and his face was covered with a long, white beard. They called him a Taoist. She smelt the fragrance of red apples and the breeze.

He smiled, looking at her face for some time, as the sun rose from the sea. His features crept close to her and he told her, "This is yours. You! Eat the pearl! Don't worry about it."

She began eating the pearl. He disappeared. That pearl was not delicious, but a little bitter. She woke up, suspicious: what was it?

She became pregnant with my brother.

(Miss Chŏng, student)

A boy is a "bitter," and appears at "sunrise."
A woman, about to conceive, returns to the place of her own birth in a dream, for she is, in a sense, about to be reborn.

GOLD

I

My mother was a poor farmer's wife, but very diligent. She was very healthy, too, and led a happy life with her husband.

In a dream, she walked over to the cotton field at the foot of a mountain, intending to gather cotton balls. Coming near, she saw a big ball of gold on the peak.

She hurriedly climbed to the top, but the glittering gold ball disappeared before she could reach it. She woke up disappointed.

She gave birth to a boy. It's me.

I was bright enough to go to elementary school at the age of four. Though very diligent, I have a quick temper.

(Mr. Nam, teacher)

A boy is "big" and glitters on "top" of a mountain.

2

My father was striding along a narrow road. All the world was dark. A dim light appeared at a distance. He ran there. It was gold. He ate it. Afterwards, he threw up what he had eaten. What he threw up changed from solid gold to liquid gold, and the liquid gold increased, growing lighter than before.

The road was clear. All the world was light. My father was surprised, and woke up.

The child was a girl. She is straight-thinking, broad-minded and runs a business.

(Miss Mun, student)

"Liquid" is *yin* and flows like a girl.

Here a *yang* trait, solid, has been transformed into a *yin* liquid. As all "spirits" are originally sexually neuter, they can be conceived as either males or females depending on their own *karma*, or past behavior (assuming they are being reborn), and on the particular attractions of their new parents' hearts. Each party gets what he or she deserves, according to the nature of his or her own thoughts and actions in this or other lives, not necessarily what he or she wants, for as the Buddhists say, "You marry your own *karma*."

Regardless, sometimes the sex of a newly conceived baby, still a shapeless egg, hangs truly in a balance and can easily fall one way or the other depending on the dream. The projections of the dreamer's own wishes, may in other words affect reality, and the baby may change sex from male to female or vice versa. In fact, Kim, Hong-kyŏng, a respected, Oriental medical doctor, believes that a child's sex is not really fixed until a few weeks after conception. He prescribes a medicine which can help effect a sexual change, desired by parents, usually in favor of a son. The mother swallows a concoction of boiled *yang* herbs to change a girl into a boy, or one of *yin* herbs for the opposite result.

COIN

I

On the way to her parents' home, my mother spotted some gold shining in the stream. My father picked it out, but it was a pack of silver coins. He gave it to her.

My eldest sister was born.
(Miss Cho, student)

"Silver coins" are gentle *yin* and buy a daughter; her father's preference in his wife's dream.

2

One sunny spring day, my mother stooped over the stream near my house washing our family's clothes. She heard a sudden splash. Astonished, she glanced around and saw an ox bathing in the stream.

After bathing, the ox lunged up on the land and disappeared in the sky. It was so mysterious that she went back to where it had been bathing. There she found a gold coin. She picked it up, clutching it to her breast.

After the dream, she became pregnant. Ten months later I, a son, was born.
(Mr. Kim, student)

A "gold coin" is *yang* and buys a son.
An "ox" disappearing "in the sky" makes him strong and magical.

HAIRPIN

My mother was trying to pick a broken silver hairpin out of a stream....
Two months after being born, my sister died.
(Anon., housewife)

The "hairpin" was the "silver" girl's vital fiber.

MAGICAL RINGS

The Venerable Haklenayasa was an itinerant monk

197

and teacher from the country of Walsi in India. After his father prayed to Buddha for a son, his mother dreamed a brightly glowing boy carried a gold ring down from the summit of Mount Sumeru (an imaginary holy mountain, the peak of which signifies return to the original state of enlightenment), and said, "I have come into my mother's dream."

(Sŏk Sŏng-u, *T'aegyo*)

A ring, here, represents one who has transcended the cycle of life and death.

In Korea, a boy receives a gold ring on his first birthday, and this custom influences rings in dreams. For instance, one woman dreamed she went to a boy's first birthday party, but his parents wouldn't accept the gold ring she had brought him as a gift, saying, "We have enough already, thank you." Consequentially, she got a daughter.

I

My mother had been wandering tired through the forest in the deep night. It was dark and cold. She was also very hungry, and lost.

Suddenly an old man with a long white beard appeared before her. He gave her a small ring and disappeared.

My mother tried to put it on, but it did not fit her finger. For a long time she tried putting it on until finally she could do so. The ring twinkled brightly. It lit up the dark forest.

Mother's friends said the effort to put the ring on meant the education of a son. He (I) would be a good man.

(Mr. Pae, student)

Such brightness is emitted by a boy.

A ring is for sincerity. Your baby will be devoted to its parents, and then, to its future spouse.

2

My mother walked to a small spring to wash some rice. When dipping out water with a gourd dipper, she found a silver ring in it. Picking it out, she put it on her finger, happy for it was the same one she had lost before.

After this she became pregnant with my older sister. She is thirty two years old now; married, and has children.

(Mrs. Che, teacher)

"Silver" is tranquil, for a girl.

Ring dreams: 56% 女, because the feminine, *yin* shape is round.

The "spirit" of a baby "lost (miscarried)" was reunited with its former mother.

WATCH

My sister-in-law was turning over rocks in a stream in a deep and unknown mountain, catching crayfish. The water was clear as crystal. While she was looking for crayfish, she saw a lady's watch underwater. It was shining like silver.

At first, she thought it must be out of order, so she could not use it. But, because of its shining, she picked it up, and checked whether or not it worked, putting it to her ear. The ticking sound was very clear; it was working very well.

After this, she woke up.

The baby was a pretty girl. She is in middle school. (Anon., student)

"A lady's watch" means a young lady is due.

"Silver," and reclusive "crayfish" also signify a girl.

HOUSEHOLD GOODS

I was guiding a group of Western men and women through the countryside. Sliding down a slope of cinders to a railroad track, before me, at the bottom of the opposite slope, I discovered a cave. Signaling the others to wait I crawled ahead, exploring.

Partly up the dark passage I came to the doorway of an Oriental livingroom and its mistress, a refined Chinese

200

lady of about forty eight years old. She cordially invited me in and showed me around her exquisite, lacquered tables of various geometric shapes and engraved chests with numerous drawers. She led me through an archway to an immaculate, smaller room, where I admired stools enladened with mother-of-pearl fishes and quiet landscapes hanging from the walls.

I then asked the lady, "Do you mind if I call my friends in for a tour of your home?"

"Of course not," she replied, quite pleased, adjusting her black bun and poking a jade peg through it. Her silvery gown was dreamily embroidered with golden birds, butterflies and flowers.

I crawled back out of the cave and called up to my friends, "Come on down for a tour of a Chinese house!"

Of course, they were eager....

Later, when I awoke, I realized my friends were members of the Association for the Study of Dreams, whom I had met at last summer's (1988) conference in California, and the house was my newly finished book of birth dreams.

(F.J. Seligson)

MAGIC HOUSE

Hui-neung (638-713) was a young woodcutter in China. One day, overhearing someone reciting a few lines of the Diamond Sutra, he suddenly became enlightened. Later, after composing a poem describing how "not-a-thing originally exists," he received transmission of the Dharma and became the sixth Patriarch of the Southern Sect of Chinese Zen Buddhism, a sect popular in Korea today.

When his mother became pregnant, she dreamed of many flowers in full blossom and birds flying around her in pairs. Also her house was permeated by a mysterious fragrance.

(Adapted from Sŏk, Sŏng-u, *T'aegyo*)

Blossoming means enlightenment. Birds in pairs is harmony. The mysterious fragrance is the scent of a holy being.

Walking along the street, I saw a tall, typical Korean house, its sloping roof covered with tiles. The house was of a grand scale. It had three large doors.

Going inside, I could see fantastic scenes; it had beautiful cliffs and a clear river. A lovely, high mountain and secluded valleys. I stayed for about an hour. I can't forget the scenery.

I had a boy. He is five years old, very affectionate, though rash and stubborn.

(Anon., teacher)

A house opening to the wide countryside is *yang*, and belongs to a free and natural boy.

LOCK AND KEY

1

An old man with a white beard appeared, and handed my mother a lock. He looked like a minister.

My sister was born. She studied theology, and is now teaching ethics in a high school.

(Mrs. Pak, Korea Women's Institute)

"A lock" is the girl friend of a key.

2

An old man with a long, white beard appeared before my mother, offering her something heavy. As soon as she

202

accepted it, he disappeared and she was surrounded by darkness.

Unwrapping the bundle, she found two golden keys in it. The more she rubbed them with her thumb, the more shiny they became. At last, they were as bright as the sun. I was born. I'm an indecisive young man of thirty. (Anon., student)

"A key" is the boy friend of a lock.

The young man can't decide which of his *yang* "keys" of life to use, or when.

CRYSTAL KITCHEN

I was visiting a country house whose roof was made of weeds. There were four clay walls in the kitchen, but they were made of crystal. Each wall had a different color: pink, white, yellow and purple, shining into each other. Surprised by such a beautiful house, I said, "I'd like to live here," to the middle-aged lady I was visiting.

She exclaimed, "Would you really like to live here? Really?" Then she took a handful of white crystal from the wall, giving it to me. It reflected on the four walls and on the ceiling.

I gave birth to a daughter.
(Woman met at a Buddhist temple)

"A kitchen" is a place to find a girl; rainbow colors are for a colorful personality.

BOWL

One day in April, 1961, my mother was invited to a dinner party at the Presidential Mansion, the Blue House, with other women chairmen of local party chapters.

After a simple ceremony, all the women chairmen were given presents by President Rhee Syng-man as rewards for service. Everyone, except my mother, was given a small, light one. But my mother's present was exceptionally big and heavy.

Greatly delighted, she hurried back home as soon as possible, untying the package. Unfortunately, it was a used silvery brass, rice bowl. The moment my mother saw it, she was very disappointed. But after hearing that the bowl had been used by the president, she took it and wrapped it up in her skirt.

Ten months later she gave birth to a pretty girl. As the girl grew older, she became more and more beautiful, growing up into a fine young woman. Receiving a bowl from the president means the girl will be honored after becoming an adult. I am she, and to my surprise, I am a teacher in a national primary school now.

(Mrs. Kim)

The bowl is womb-like; one more "silvery" girl's mouth to feed. A dream of a crystal glass or cup also describes a girl's organ.

SPOON

While my mother was washing clothes in a river, she saw something shining at the bottom. Though wanting to get at it, she couldn't because the river was very deep.

Soon the object began rising upwards till she could grasp it. It was a silver spoon, shining very brightly.

Ten months later she gave birth to me, a son.

They say, "Brightness indicates cleverness, and you will be good to others because a spoon is used for serving food."

(Mr. An, student)

A spoon is phallic. A boy's energy rises up on its own accord.

PILLOWS

In the state of Ch'in in China, a lady dreamt of two lovely pillows lying on her bed. Light was coming out of them, and they blended together in the form of the moon.

She gave birth to twin girls. They both later became wives of King Hsien-kung (who ruled 678-? B.C.).

(Mrs. Wang Su-yi, professor)

The twins, forming one moon, perhaps would not be jealous of each other.

COMB AND MIRROR

While my mother was combing her hair in front of a mirror, a black dog was gazing at her from the far left, its eyes glittering.

Mother's combing her hair in front of a mirror meant a girl. I am quick and stubborn, a bit of a tomboy. I've been working at a bank for ten years.

(Miss Kim, teller)

A girl likes the *yin,* "left" side.
"Glittering eyes" belong to a tomboy.

NEEDLE

My mother was traveling on a train, and noticed a box near her. Peeking inside, she saw it was full of sewing needles, precious and gold. Desiring it very much, she hid it, worried somebody else might see it, and, after, carried it home.

She had a girl.

(Lady at Korea Women's Institute)

A "needle" is bisexual: male, due to its long, sharp point, and female, because its eye is a hole. However, the fact that sewing needles are used primarily by females gravitates the child to her sex.

"Gold," here, means skill at sewing.

SHOES

My mother visited a church, and found various shoes there. She said, "I would be so happy if all of these were mine."

While she was looking at them lovingly, a clergyman came out. "Good afternoon," he said. "Good afternoon," she replied. And he told her, "Take a few pairs of shoes."

My mother chose a pair of black rubber shoes and a pair of pretty high-heels. Then she felt a lump in her throat, and wished to return home in a hurry, so as to wear her shoes.

When she got into the house, she tried on her black rubber shoes, and stored the pretty high heels in a garret.

Ten months after, she became my mother. And three years later, my sister was born. That is to say, the black rubber shoes are me, and the pretty high-heels my sister.

(Miss Hah, student)

"Women's shoes" yield girls; here, one practical and one stylish.

SILK

My mother was lost in the forest, so she tried to get back home, but could not find the way. A long time later, she came upon a road covered with white silk. She followed it; the air was full of dawn mist. After a long walk

206

on this silk road, she arrived at a temple, stopping by the front door. Suddenly an old man with white hair and a long white beard appeared from nowhere.

She made a respectful salutation with her clasped hands. Then he said, "You will have a son. Take good care of him. He can be a great figure some day."

She mumbled, "Thank you, thank you," bowing again, and awoke.

A few days later I was born. I am a man, not good, not bad.

(Anon., student)

A "son" wrapped in "white silk" is shiny and pure.

THREAD

One night, my mother wandered through the fields to a quiet patch of beans. Finding a bright, white spool of thread in a furrow, she brought it back home.

Five months later, she gave birth to a daughter, me. So she says my life will be very long, and I'll be a pure woman in society.

(Miss Won, teacher)

A furrow is a cavity, for a fruitful girl.
The longer and whiter the "thread," the longer her life.

ODDS AND ENDS

INK BRUSH

Ch'eng-kung was ruler (663-? B.C.) of the Chinese state of Ch'in. One of the most interesting parts of his life took place before his birth: His mother dreamt that a god came before her and, with a calligraphy brush, painted a baby's hip black.

Afterwards, when her child was born he really did have a big, black birth mark on his hip.

(Wang Su-yi, professor)

While my mother was climbing up to the top of a mountain, she noticed something glittering, half buried in the ground. It was a shining box. Opening it, she discovered a golden writing brush and some pieces of rice paper inside. Taking them with her, she climbed back down.

So I was born. I am meditative.

(Mr. Kim, student)

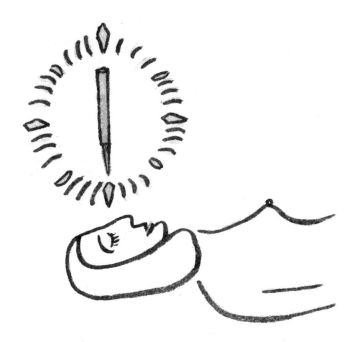

A calligraphy brush is for your budding scholar or painter.

"A brush" is a phallus.
"Golden" is a sign of a "shining" scholar.

PENCIL

A big, long yellow snake suddenly slithered quietly into the room. My mother was surprised to see the monster. It looked like a dragon. She stopped breathing and kept watching.

It began crawling slowly up onto a small desk. Soon it was making a circle with its body and mother kept watching it. In the middle of the coil, its head came out. It bit at a pencil, holding it in its mouth, and began writing letters. But my mother couldn't understand their meanings. Then the snake crept silently out of the room.

She woke up, sweat all over her body. Shaking her husband, she told him the dream, and he was very pleased.

So she used to tell me, "You will be a great scholar in the future."

(Mr. Chang, teacher)

CLOCK

My mother had a strange clock—a very, very strange clock. She concealed it in her bosom and many people came to see that clock. But she hid it from them.

After this dream, she bore a son, me.

Sensitive and introverted, I like being alone.

(Mr. Ch'oe, student)

A clock is the male counterpart of a smaller watch.

HAMMER

I met an old man by a stream. He said, "In the big mountain you can find some lumber." So I clambered up the mountain. It was difficult. A river was coursing by. Coming closer, I found it frozen. Under the ice was an iron hammer and some wood. Breaking the ice, I lifted them out, and returned home.

I had a son. He likes to make things using tools and is good at repairs. He has a gentle personality, and is in middle school.

(Lady at Korea Women's Institute)

A hammer is long with a knobby head, as is a boy's organ.

SWORD

My mother saw a tall, brave admiral, who was grasping a big, shining sword, while commanding sailors in a fleet sailing through the sea.

Friends guessed the sword symbolized power. Mother prayed for this dream to come true. The baby, a boy, really did grow up to be active and brave like a great general of the future. He was cheerful, and good at baseball, and an excellent fighter. But later he twice failed the exam for entering the Military Academy two times, and decided to attend a regular university. He now wants to be a reporter.

(Mr. Pak, student)

As the admiral was male, so was the child. Maybe he should have applied to the Naval Academy!

TRICYCLE

My mother was riding a tiny tricycle up a hill behind her village. Though trying to get to the top, she thought it would be impossible, because the road was so narrow and steep.

Miraculously, as soon as she rode onto the sloping road, it became broad and flat. Reaching the end of the flat road, she saw another slanting one. It also turned into an even road as soon as she got to it. So she could gain the top of the mountain easily.

The Three Magi from the Orient, who had celebrated the birth of the baby Jesus Christ, were waiting for her. They gave her a peaceful benediction.

I, a boy, was born.

(Mr. Pyŏn, student)

The tricycle hints of a boy. The sloping road's changing into a broad, flat one means he will be able to get over the adversities of life. Gaining the top of the mountain inspires the boy to seek a high position. The blessing of the Magi suggests he will contribute to the welfare of the world.

KOREAN FLAGS

One day, my mother washed our family's clothes, and hung them on the line to dry. As soon as she did so, they all changed into flags, *T'aegŭkki*.

After this, she gave birth to my younger brother. He is smart, and in high school. So my mother says, "He will be a great man for our country."

(Anon., student)

The Korean flag, *T'aegŭkki,* containing the round, *yin* and *yang,* symbol of Taoism and Confucianism,—represents all the inter-play of female and male qualities in nature; that's why her child will be so great!

Part Six

AN INTERPRETATION
OF BIRTH DREAMS

You consult the diviner of dreams:
They all say: we are wise;
But who can distinguish the male and female
crow?

(The Book of Poetry, Legge trs.)

In light of my collection of over 2000 birth dreams, one can come closer to realizing the traditional belief that about "80% of all birth dreams *(t'aemong)* come true." Tools for interpretation include folk beliefs, *yin/yang* aspects, and dream body behavior.

FOLK BELIEFS

The twelve Oriental Zodiac animals (Mouse, Cow, Tiger, Rabbit, Dragon, Snake, Horse, Goat, Monkey, Chicken, Dog and Pig) can suggest what personality to expect of a child born on such an animal's dream, doubly so if it occurs, as is common, during the cyclical years of the animal in question (e.g., 1989, the Year of the Snake). In the following dream all the Zodiac animals ("gods") appear:

One night, while my mother was counting stars in the dark sky,

215

a comet shot down nearby. She strode to the spot, and peeking behind a tree found a smiling baby.

Soon twelve people with various animals' masks on their faces appeared around the baby, and with a severe wind blowing all over, joyfully celebrated the baby's birth. My mother was absorbed in the singing and dancing without being detected behind the tree.

At daybreak, they disappeared, and the baby was left alone. My mother crept up close, and hugged it.

She named me "Hyŏng-je," which means "Brother," because those gods and I enjoyed ourselves as if we were brothers. I have a calm and easy-going nature.

(Mr. Shin, student)

Folk beliefs as to the sex of a baby symbol can be discerned by comparing a wealth of dreams from various dreamers, as I have done below. This chart gives us forty-five sample baby symbols appearing in my dream collection, and the number of times the babies turned out to be boys or girls. The percentages of each are listed and from these we can divine the probability of a boy or girl being born based on the name of a symbol alone. An outstanding characteristic of children presaged by each of these symbols is given.

Symbol	Boys (男)	Girls (女)	Character
Sun	23(79%)	6(21%)	glorious
Moon	20(57%)	15(43%)	luminous
Star	19(66%)	10(34%)	brilliant
Flower	18(13%)	124(87%)	lovely
Apple	6(17%)	29(83%)	cheerful
Cherry	0(0%)	5(100%)	provocative
Cucumber	5(56%)	4(44%)	humorous
Date	5(100%)	0(0%)	stoic
Grape	4(100%)	0(0%)	sensuous
Peach	25(47%)	28(53%)	sweet
Persimmon	21(68%)	10(32%)	joyful
Strawberry	0(0%)	6(100%)	hearty

AN INTERPRETATION OF BIRTH DREAMS

Symbol	Boys (男)	Girls (女)	Character
Chestnut	40(50%)	40(50%)	soft-hearted
Walnut	6(86%)	1(14%)	intelligent
Ginseng	9(82%)	2(18%)	vital
Pepper	39(72%)	15(28%)	hot-tempered
Potato	7(78%)	2(22%)	light-colored
Pumpkin	7(58%)	5(32%)	fertile
Radish	12(92%)	1(08%)	persistent
Butterfly	1(14%)	6(86%)	whimsical
Carp	27(69%)	12(31%)	ambitious
Goldfish	4(40%)	6(60%)	dainty
Shellfish	3(30%)	7(70%)	chaste
Dragon	143(84%)	28(16%)	ambitious
Snake	122(59%)	84(41%)	clever
Toad	4(40%)	6(60%)	sluggish
Turtle	17(81%)	4(19%)	patient
Crane	11(79%)	3(21%)	pure
Eagle	5(100%)	0(0%)	lofty
Owl	0(0%)	2(100%)	jolly
Peacock	5(83%)	1(17%)	showy
Bear	8(88%)	1(12%)	protective
Deer	3(43%)	4(57%)	gentle
Lion	7(88%)	1(12%)	fierce
Rabbit	2(25%)	6(75%)	playful
Tiger	109(81%)	26(19%)	ferocious
Hen	2(29%)	5(71%)	meticulous
Rooster	6(86%)	1(14%)	proud
Cow	45(80%)	11(20%)	docile
Horse	12(71%)	5(29%)	lusty
Pig	89(76%)	28(24%)	rich
Jewel	5(33%)	13(67%)	showy
Ring	17(44%)	22(56%)	possessive
Spoon	10(76%)	3(24%)	generous
Watch	0(0%)	6(100%)	punctual

With dreams such as of cherries, strawberries and watches for girls, or grapes, dates and bears for boys, where so far, no exceptions as to a designated sex have occurred, the sex of a unborn child can be guessed at, but

217

our statistical sample is small. With other symbols like flowers and apples representing girls, or dragons and tigers for boys, where our sample is bigger and the percentages remarkably high, a dreamer can be reasonably sure of what the sex is going to be.

But, one should never depend on such a superficial judgement (as is commonly made by housewives insufficiently schooled in the old lore), based on the name of the symbol alone, because each species of dream symbol contains both a male and a female gender. Rather, a greater probability may usually be intuited by considering, in addition, the following *yin* and *yang* aspects of a dream.

YIN / YANG ASPECTS

According to aspects of color, time, space, number, or other physical qualities, based on a prevalence of cases, a dream symbol tends to be female or male. Ambiguous dreams account for the births of effeminate boys and tomboy girls.

For colors, the distinction is often not by color, but by shade; whether the dream object is *yang*, radiating bright like the sun, a sparkling diamond, or a glowing tiger's eye for a boy; or comparatively *yin*, shadowy such as birdlike clouds, books in a cave, or even a castle under the sea for a girl.

In case by case, according to custom, dream objects of similar colors may represent different sexes. For example, a sour, green fruit (apple) foretells a boy, but a cool, green vegetable (pepper), a girl. A hot, red vegetable (pepper) is for a boy, but a sweet, red fruit (apple), a girl. This is because *yin/yang* aspects of sweet for girl and sour for boy, and hot for boy and cool for girl override color in the choice of sex.

Also, colors may tell us something about the character of a future child. Thus rainbow colors (on books in an attic, on walls of a kitchen) are for an artistic girl. Red (cherry on a cliff) is for a passionate girl. Blue (orchid) a virtuous boy; and yellow (melon under water) a generous girl. A fresh black skin of a vegetable (eggplant) or animal (dragon) indicates a sensual and pliable person, or even a future Taoist sage. However, an unnaturally dull color (on a black hairpin) may warn of ill fortune, possibly even death.

The soft white skin of a fruit (peach) or animal (horse) may symbolize a virtuous girl or even an austere, sword-bearing warrior. Or the glowing white hair of a god may announce a holy child.

Girls, being shy, tend to seek the cover of night (owl), when they won't be seen; and boys, being bold, grace the light of day (eagle). A Korean word for wife, *ansaram,* means "inside person;" and that for the husband, *pakkatsaram*, is "outside person." The man traditionally works outside the house, perhaps in the fields with the ox, and the woman works within, cooking or sewing. Thus girl symbols reside indoors (a persimmon in a glass cabinet), and boys romp outdoors (a dog roaming the hills). Also, boys favor the right side (lion biting shoulder); and girls, the left (dog staring at mother).

Furthermore, a boy symbol's *yang* energy surges up like a geyser, as when making love (dragon flying to heaven). A girl's *yin,* having no force of its own, slides down like rain or a waterfall with the flow of gravity (jewel at the bottom of a stream). More specifically, symbols for boys are found in such places as on mountaintops (ball of gold), and symbols for girls on precipices. A cliff is analogous to the female cleft and the receptive potentiality of emptiness:

> My mother saw a graceful deer loping up a dangerous cliff. It was rough, and the deer looked lonely. She felt sympathy for it.
> She had a daughter, me. I am kind and open-minded.
> (Miss Lee, teacher)

Numbers of dream objects: "zero" (like a seedless mandarin orange) is for a girl, for she can have an vacant womb:

> My mother was hiking through a large field with her husband and mother-in-law. There were many beautiful flowers in the field and she was very happy. After walking merrily for a long time, they saw many red peppers. Her mother-in-law said, "Pick them and take them home." But my mother said, "I can't pick them, they aren't ours. We mustn't pick them." They continued arguing this way, and finally, returned home without any red peppers.
> When she had a baby, it was a daughter, me. If she had listened to my grandmother, perhaps she would have had a son.
> (Miss Son, teacher)

"One" (especially one long seed, as in a date or grain of rice) is a boy, because his penis counts as "one."

> My mother was walking in a field. A solitary persimmon hung from a tree. She admired the fruit, eager to have it. Suddenly an old man with quite a long beard appeared, and spoke to her, "That persimmon is mine. I'll give it to you, but you can't have all the seeds. Give me back the seeds."
> My mother ate the persimmon, but kept one of three seeds.
> She said, "If I'd kept all the seeds, I would have had three sons," but she had only one.
> (Anon., teacher)

"Half" (half moon), and "split in two" (oyster, butterfly

or harelip; split fruits and vegetables) are for a girl, since she is open to receive and bear life.

My aunt walked to the river to do some washing. The water was clean and calm. While washing dresses, she saw many petals in the water. They were floating down stream, and she plucked them out of the water.

On her way home with the petals, she picked up a pumpkin on the road, but it slipped out of her arms, splitting in two.

She had a modest and polite girl.

(Mrs. Kim, teacher)

"Two" may be for twins (pumpkin girls, or ginseng boys).

"Three" (stars or potatoes) is often for a boy, as a penis and testicles count as "three." But it also has various mystical meanings, like the Taoist, combined graces of "Heaven (god), Earth (god) and Man (god)," and could be either an auspicious boy or girl.

"Two, three, four, etc.,..." may mean the total number of a mother's future children.

My mother says, "The water of our well was as clear as crystal. I fished three spoons and two brown pieces of seaweed out of it. Afterwards, I had three sons and two daughters."

(Mrs. Hwang, teacher)

"Many" (seeds) may mean a girl, since girls are fertile.

Other qualities of dream symbols: small and weak (goldfish) are typically a girl; big and strong (carp) a boy. Long, phallic (radish), is typically a boy; womb-shaped (swan or cup), a girl, and so on, usually corresponding to Freud's notions, but with cultural variations. A "thin" or "small" snake is almost always a girl, for it is analogous in the folk mind to the clitoris, which resembles a "rudi-

A carrot is for dedication and masculinity. Your child will stick at any task until it is completed.

mentary penis." For instance an old woman who lives near our home told my wife, "A small yellow snake crept under my knees and into my vagina. I had a daughter."

By contrast a "big" or "long" snake is usually a boy.

Flowers are for girls, not due to color, but because they are soft and dainty.

DREAM BODY BEHAVIOR

The more wild, fast and aggressive (a biting lion) the dream baby's behavior, especially if towards the father, or intimate with the mother (making love with Samson), the more likely the baby will be a boy. This behavior reflects the natural competition, as in the West, of son with father for the affection of mother.

The more tame, slow and shy, or less intimate the dream baby is with the mother (a following lion), or if more close to the father (stroking an elephant), the more likely the baby will be a girl. This behavior evidences a natural attraction of daughter to father and vice versa.

A girl, though usually affectionate, may bite her mother (twin snakes biting her breasts). A lady, also, sitting before a mirror, putting on make up or jewelry, fancy clothes or high heels, or going shopping for such items, often, promises a girl.

Beyond this, the relations of the dreamer and the dreamed, whether loving or combative, deceitful or honest, begrudging or accepting, are likely, unless the dreamer strives otherwise, to set a pattern for their relations after the child is born. The dream instills or reflects a bias, which echoes back and forth between the thoughts of the dreamer and the delicate foetal mind long after it is over.

Mr. Han Kŏn-dŏk, in *Dream Prophecy and Judgement,* offers birth dreamers guidance for a favorable dream:

"One, the baby symbol must not be damaged, or injured.

Two, you should make sure you completely own it, or at least keep an eye on it.

Three, do not go close to or touch it.

Four, do not go away.

Five, do not damage, injure or interfere with it.

Six, do not lose it.

Seven, do not give it to others.

Eight, you must feel satisfied with it.
Nine, the object must be marvelous or mysterious.
Ten, the conclusion of the dream must be pleasant.
Eleven, your wish must be fulfilled in the dream."

Generally I agree with Mr. Han, except for number Three, "Do not go close to or touch it." If the closeness is with affection (hugging and kissing), it may portend or foster a good relationship between the baby and dreamer. Also, I would add, "Don't steal it (Buddha statue, jewels, etc.)," for what one steals, out of desperation for a baby (usually a son) or jealousy over the baby of another, tends to drift away again.

Occasionally a woman wishing to have a boy, dreaming of a girl, or vice versa, tries to abort the child. However, Mr. Han cautions,

"You should not abort a baby because of a dream. It's not such a good way. Even when a *t'aemong* appears to have a deep meaning, it may prove to be nothing when we interpret it. On the other hand, even if we have a routine dream, it might give a rosy picture when interpreted, so a correct interpretation is very important when it comes to a *t'aemong*.

"Furthermore, a *t'aemong* shows the fluctuations of a baby's life, its high and low points. Therefore, it is easy to fall into the mistake of believing that a dream shows a whole future life, when it only shows part. If we attribute a whole life to a dream, we might be unduly pessimistic for a baby, when, in fact, maybe we haven't remembered clearly or interpreted correctly.

"So if you have a bad dream indicating that the baby's future isn't going to be rosy, it's better to forget it. But if you have a rosy dream, it's better to believe it and visualize it, and encourage the baby to reach the dream's goal."

Birth dreams are not always auspicious. At times the baby symbol dies (cut up snake), or is hurt (broken hairpin, decayed vegetable), or goes away (roaming tiger). And sad reality may coincide with a dream:

> My uncle gave ginseng roots to my mother and my aunt. As a matter of fact, both were pregnant. My mother's ginseng was fresh and green. But my aunt's was spoiled.
> After a few months my mother gave birth to me. My aunt also gave birth, but her girl died of an unknown cause.
> So the fresh ginseng was me, and the spoiled one my dead cousin.
> (Miss Kim, student)

In the face of a sad dream, it is better to follow Mr. Han's advice: take care of one's health and pray for the best. Here's an example of a not so "rosy" picture which gets better over time:

> A white hen appeared before my mother in a dream. It was very beautiful, so, passing her hand over its back, she stroked its feathers. Soon, however, a white pimple broke out on her hand. She thought this very strange.
> About ten months after, my sister was born with nothing particularly wrong with her. But a few years later, white pimples, like in the dream, erupted all over her legs. She experienced much discomfort.
> My sister now is safe and healthy. She has a feeling heart, and is a hard-working businesswoman.
> (Mrs. Chang, teacher)

ORIENTAL BIRTH DREAMS

Baby baby,
first you
were nothing,
then just
something,
only an essence,
merely a soul

from "there"
to "here,"
not even
a shadow;
from "this"
to "other,"
barely an outline

yet
in between
a vision
in my sleep:
a cat,
a pearl,
a star,
or flower,
a changing
image
of my dreams....

EPILOGUE

In the autumn of '77, I flew to Seoul from Kyoto, Japan with an old violin under my arm and only $100.00 in my pocket. I'd come to meet a girl with whom I'd been exchanging dozens of "love letters," but whom I'd seen only through a single photograph; her hair parted in the middle and tied back traditionally. She was bedecked in a billowy Korean dress, and standing half hidden behind some pink and white cosmos flowers.

She greeted me at Kimpo airport and, with a big, silent smile, whisked me off in a taxi to her little, secluded room. A few months later, while it was snowing in the mountains, we were wed in a Buddhist temple, with the blessings of her parents.

My wife told me,

"My mother's parents had a big farm and a spacious, traditional-style house, always filled with many people. She was the youngest of eleven children, and so a bit spoiled. She had wanted to go off to art school in Tokyo after graduation from high school, for her teacher had offered her a scholarship. But one night, in a dream, she found herself in her classroom, and a great, blue dragon was outside the windows, trying to get in. She screamed, fleeing to the front door to escape, but as she opened it, the dragon was waiting for her there, too.

"The next morning, she learned that a marriage had been arranged for her to someone she didn't even know. He was a distant member of the royal family, whose symbol was a blue dragon, and who had just graduated

227

from mining school. Soon after the marriage took place she found herself in a little house up in the forests of Kŭm-gang Mountain, in the north, wondering if she was going to have a birth dream. When she had one, and then another and so on for each of her children, she would recognize it immediately. It was not an ordinary dream, for it was so fresh and beautiful. It was only from the dream that she first learned that she was pregnant, for up there in the mountain there was no doctor to tell her, and the child would be delivered by a midwife in her own house. She had birth dreams for all of her children, and all of them came true:

"For her first child, she dreamed of walking in the countryside and coming to a very beautiful tree full of ripe persimmons. But they were too high for her to reach, though she wished to have one. Then a bird flew up, knocking a persimmon off the branch and into her hands. She took it home, and set it behind a glass cabinet window. It was very lovely, but she couldn't touch it; she could only look at it and admire it.

"My older sister was born. She was very beautiful, just like a persimmon. She grew up, talented in Chinese embroidery and Korean harp, but held herself aloof from others in the family, just like the persimmon behind the glass. During her last year, just before leaving home, she was kind to me. She became a nun, but not long after passed away....

"For her next child, my mother dreamed of approaching a very large peach on a tree in an orchard. Standing on her tiptoes, she reached up and picked it off. Carrying it home, she set it down on the kitchen table, intending to eat it. So she cut it open with a knife, but to her dismay, it was completely rotten.

"Later, a handsome boy was born, and my grandfather declared, 'He'll be a star (General).' But before reaching 100 days old (a traditional safe point after childbirth), he died.

"While my mother was pregnant with me, she dreamed of walking by a very lovely pond. Then she found a field of white lilies-of-the-valley. She sat down and with some scissors cut only three. She wrapped them in her skirt, carrying them home, but on the way she worried, 'They are so few!'

"Of course, white lilies meant a pure girl, but she feared only three were for a short life. I nearly died while escaping in my mother's arms from Seoul during the Korean War, then again, of smallpox in Pusan, so maybe by now my luck has changed.

"While my mother was dreaming of my youngest sister, she was walking through a wide field of all kinds of wildflowers. Sitting down on the ground, she started snipping off flowers with some scissors, collecting them in her lap. Then she took them up, wrapping them in her *ch'ima* (ample Korean skirt) and began to hurry home, for she was troubled about something. Glancing behind her, she saw a lion. It followed her quietly through the flowers and she kept glancing back.

"The flowers meant a girl, and the lion suggested my sister would have a leonine character. In fact, she is very strong and outgoing. She was president of her coed high school class and played the trumpet in the brass band. We call her, 'Lion Sister.'"

Intrigued by the mysterious coincidence of these lovely dreams, I asked my students at the Hankuk University of

Foreign Studies and the primary and secondary school teachers in my vacation, teacher training workshops to fill out questionnaires in English. They read, "Using the dreamer's own words, tell the whole story of a birth dream, yours or that of somebody close to you. Give the sex, personality and present occupation of the child born."

Nearly all of their births were heralded by wondrous dreams. I collected these dreams for over seven years, until I had more than 2000 of them, representing all regions of Korea.

I am now gathering dreams of birth, marriage and death from countries around the world. If the reader wishes to send me any such dreams she or he has had I will gratefully read them.

F. J. Seligson
H.U.F.S.,E.E.
270 Imun-dong
Seoul, 131-791, Korea

Paradise*

Mr. Seligson got lost on his way to school.

We were very surprised this morning, because Mr. Seligson didn't appear at our class; he is a very diligent, precise man. We made a phone call to Mrs. Seligson. She was surprised at the news. She said, "He went out early this morning. What happened to him?" And suddenly, she burst into tears.

At last, Mr. Seligson appeared at sunset. His hair and clothes were terribly messed up. He explained what had happened:

He was strolling to the bus stop to go to school this morning, when he found a strange hole under the street. His curiosity made him check it out and he suddenly fell into the hole.

A paradise, a fantastic world was there. Many foetuses were living there, waiting for birth, and the *Samshin Halmŏ-ni* (Birth Grandmother) took care of them all. She made their birth and fate there. Mr. Seligson was very interested in it. He tried to ask her about *t'aemong* (birth dreams). "..."

At that very moment he felt that somebody was shaking him, "Wake up! Wake up! This is the bus terminal. You have to get off now. Hurry up!"

---

* By Ko, E.S., Lee, K.M., Pae, M.H., Kim, H.R., Im, E.W., and Saw, Y.K., my students.

REFERENCES

Articles about Korea

Furuta, Hiroshi, "Dreamy Korea," In *Language,* vol. 15, no 11, (Tokyo: Taishikan, 1986) (In Japanese)

Kim Young-tae, M.D., "Study of Traditional Taboos During Pregnancy in Yŏju, Kyŏnggi-do," Korea University, Graduate School of Medicine (thesis), 1985 (In Korean)

Lee Kyu-dong, M.D., "Psychoanalytical Studies on *T'aemong,"* in *Modern Medicine* 5 : 5 , November, 1966 (In Korean)

Moon H.S., M.D., "A Study on *T'aemong"* Seoul National University, Graduate School of Medicine (thesis) 26 : 4, 1974 (In Korean)

Rhi Bou-yong, M.D., "Archetypal Images of the Korean," in *Psychology News* 8 : 1, Supplement, 1984 (In Korean)

Seligson, Fred Jeremy, "Traditional Korean Birth Dreams." *Korea Journal,* December, 1987 (Seoul : UNESCO). "Les reves presages de conception," *Revue de Coree,* Spring, 1988 (Seoul : UNESCO)

Books about Korea

Anonymous, *Un-gae Pillow,* (as part of the Chosen Sotokuhu, Showa 19) (In Japanese)

Cha Jae-ho, Chung Bom-mo, and Lee Sung-jin, "Boy Preference Reflected in Korean Folklore," *Virtues in Conflict,* edited by Mattielli, Sandra, (Seoul: R.A.S. 1977)

Han Kŏn-dŏk, *Dream Prophecy and Judgement,* (Seoul: Myŏng-mundang, 1983) (In Korean)

Ilyŏn, *Samguk Yusa,* English edition translated by Ha Tae-hung and Grafton K. Mintz, (Seoul: Yonsei University Press, 1972). Korean edition translated from the original Chinese by Lee, Man-sin (Seoul: Eul-Yoo Publishing Co., Ltd., 1975)

Kim Pu-shik, *Samguk Sagi*, translated by Kim, C.K. (Seoul: Taeyang Publishing Co., 1972)

Lee Ki-baik, *A New History of Korea,* translated by Edward W. Wagner with Edward J. Shultz (Seoul: Ilchokak Publishers, 1984)

Park Young-jun, compiler, *Traditional Tales of Old Korea,* (Seoul: Han-guk Munhwa Pub. Co., 1974)

Sŏk Sŏng-u, *T'aegyo* (Fetal Education): "The Door of Pregnancy" (Seoul: Paegyang Pub. Co., 1986) (In Korean)

Books about China

Anonymous, *Collection of All Books from Ancient Times Until Now (Ch'ing Dynasty Government 1644-1911)* (In Chinese)

Anonymous, *Chinese Mythology,* (Taipei: Huh Luoa Pub. Co., 1976) (In Chinese)

Gong, Pung-Chung, and Chang, Hua-Ching, *A Collection on the History of the Chinese Novel,* (Taipei: Taiwan Student's Bookstore, 1984) (In Chinese)

In Dong-Goa, *The Story of Emperors,* (Taipei: World Art Pub. Co., 1987) (In Chinese)

Legge, James, translation of volume IV of *The Chinese Classics, The Book of Poetry (She King),* (Hong Kong: Hong Kong University Press, 1960)

Mackenzie, Donald A., *Myths of China and Japan,* (Boston: Longwood Press, 1923)

Needham, Joseph, *Science and Civilization in China,* (Cambridge University Press, 1956), vol. II.

Veith, Ilza, *The Yellow Emperor's Classic of Internal Medicine,* (Berkeley: University of California Press, 1949)

Wang Sher-Jeun, *Chinese Myths About People,* (Taipei: Star Pub. Co., 1985) (In Chinese)

Werner, E.T.C., *A Dictionary of Chinese Mythology,* (Shanghai: Kelly and Walsh, 1932)

Wieger, Leo, *A History of the Religious Beliefs and Philosophi-*

cal Opinions in China, (Werner, E.T.C., trs.) (Shanghai: Hsien-hsien Press, 1927)

Books about the West

Artemidorus, *The Interpretation of Dreams,* translated by Robert J. White, (New Jersey: Noyes Press, 1975)

De Becker, Raymond, *The Understanding of Dreams,* (London: George Allen and Unwin, 1968)

Lincoln, J.S., *The Dream in Primitive Cultures,* (Baltimore: Williams and Wilkins, 1935)

Steward, Kenneth M., "The Yumans," *The Handbook of North American Indians,* vol. 10 (Washington D.C.: Smithsonian Institution, 1983)

Woods, Ralph L., *The World of Dreams,* (Boston: Houghton Mifflin, 1947)

Others

Eliade, Mircea, *Shamanism: Archaic Techniques of Ecstasy,* translated by Willard Trask, (Princeton University Press, 1972)

Rhys Davids, T.W. (trs.), *Buddhist Birth Stories,* (New York: Arno Press, 1977)

INDEX

Alphabetical Dream Symbols

Biographical Dreams and Myths